JAMESTOWN EDUCATION

Timed Readings Plus *in Science*

25 Two-Part Lessons
with Questions for
Building Reading Speed and Comprehension

BOOK 6

Glencoe McGraw-Hill

New York, New York   Columbus, Ohio   Chicago, Illinois   Peoria, Illinois   Woodland Hills, California

JAMESTOWN EDUCATION

Glencoe/McGraw-Hill

A Division of The McGraw·Hill Companies

ISBN: 0-07-827375-7

Send all queries to:
Glencoe/McGraw-Hill
8787 Orion Place
Columbus, OH 43240-4027

3 4 5 6 7 8 9 10 021 08 07 06 05

CONTENTS

You probably talk at an average rate of about 150 words a minute. If you are a reader of average ability, you read at a rate of about 250 words a minute. So your reading speed is nearly twice as fast as your speaking or listening speed. This example shows that reading is one of the fastest ways to get information.

The purpose of this book is to help you increase your reading rate and understand what you read. The 25 lessons in this book will also give you practice in reading science articles and in preparing for tests in which you must read and understand nonfiction passages within a certain time limit.

Reading Faster and Better

Following are some strategies that you can use to read the articles in each lesson.

Previewing

Previewing before you read is a very important step. This helps you to get an idea of what a selection is about and to recall any previous knowledge you have about the subject. Here are the steps to follow when previewing.

Read the title. Titles are designed not only to announce the subject but also to make the reader think. Ask yourself questions such as What can I learn from the title? What thoughts does it bring to mind?

What do I already know about this subject?

Read the first sentence. If they are short, read the first two sentences. The opening sentence is the writer's opportunity to get your attention. Some writers announce what they hope to tell you in the selection. Some writers state their purpose for writing; others just try to get your attention.

Read the last sentence. If it is short, read the final two sentences. The closing sentence is the writer's last chance to get ideas across to you. Some writers repeat the main idea once more. Some writers draw a conclusion—this is what they have been leading up to. Other writers summarize their thoughts; they tie all the facts together.

Skim the entire selection. Glance through the selection quickly to see what other information you can pick up. Look for anything that will help you read fluently and with understanding. Are there names, dates, or numbers? If so, you may have to read more slowly.

Reading for Meaning

Here are some ways to make sure you are making sense of what you read.

Build your concentration. You cannot understand what you read if you are not concentrating. When you discover that your thoughts are straying, correct the situation right away. Avoid distractions and distracting situations. Keep in mind the information you learned from previewing. This will help focus your attention on the selection.

Read in thought groups. Try to see meaningful combinations of words—phrases, clauses, or sentences. If you look at only one word at a time (called word-by-word reading), both your comprehension and your reading speed suffer.

Ask yourself questions. To sustain the pace you have set for yourself and to maintain a high level of concentration and comprehension, ask yourself questions such as What does this mean? or How can I use this information? as you read.

Finding the Main Ideas

The paragraph is the basic unit of meaning. If you can quickly discover and understand the main idea of each paragraph, you will build your comprehension of the selection.

Find the topic sentence. The topic sentence, which contains the main idea, often is the first sentence of a paragraph. It is followed by sentences that support, develop, or explain the main idea. Sometimes a topic sentence comes at the end of a paragraph. When it does, the supporting details come first, building the base for the topic sentence. Some paragraphs do not have a topic sentence; all of the sentences combine to create a meaningful idea.

Understand paragraph structure. Every well-written paragraph has a purpose. The purpose may be to inform, define, explain or illustrate. The purpose should always relate to the main idea and expand on it. As you read each paragraph, see how the body of the paragraph tells you more about the main idea.

Relate ideas as you read. As you read the selection, notice how the writer puts together ideas. As you discover the relationship between the ideas, the main ideas come through quickly and clearly.

Mastering Reading Comprehension

Reading fast is not useful if you don't remember or understand what you read. The two exercises in Part A provide a check on how well you have understood the article.

Recalling Facts

These multiple-choice questions provide a quick check to see how well you recall important information from the article. As you learn to apply the reading strategies described earlier, you should be able to answer these questions more successfully.

Understanding Ideas

These questions require you to think about the main ideas in the article. Some main ideas are stated in the article; others are not. To answer some of the questions, you need to draw conclusions about what you read.

The five exercises in Part B require multiple answers. These exercises provide practice in applying comprehension and critical-thinking skills that you can use in all your reading.

Recognizing Words in Context

Always check to see whether the words around an unfamiliar word—its context—can give you a clue to the word's meaning. A word generally appears in a context related to its meaning.

Suppose, for example, that you are unsure of the meaning of the word *expired* in the following passage:

> Vera wanted to check out a book, but her library card had expired. She had to borrow my card, because she didn't have time to renew hers.

You could begin to figure out the meaning of *expired* by asking yourself a question such as, What could have happened to Vera's library card that would make her need to borrow someone else's card? You might realize that if Vera had to renew her card, its usefulness must have come to an end or run out. This would lead you to conclude that the word *expired* must mean "to come to an end" or "to run out." You would be right. The context suggested the meaning.

Context can also affect the meaning of a word you already know. The word *key,* for instance, has many meanings. There are musical keys, door keys, and keys to solving

a mystery. The context in which the word *key* occurs will tell you which meaning is correct.

Sometimes a word is explained by the words that immediately follow it. The subject of a sentence and your knowledge about that subject might also help you determine the meaning of an unknown word. Try to decide the meaning of the word *revive* in the following sentence:

> Sunshine and water will revive those drooping plants.

The compound subject is *sunshine* and *water*. You know that plants need light and water to survive and that drooping plants are not healthy. You can figure out that *revive* means "to bring back to health."

Distinguishing Fact from Opinion

Every day you are called upon to sort out fact and opinion. Because much of what you read and hear contains both facts and opinions, you need to be able to tell the two apart.

Facts are statements that can be proved true. The proof must be objective and verifiable. You must be able to check for yourself to confirm a fact.

Look at the following facts. Notice that they can be checked for accuracy and confirmed. Suggested sources for verification appear in parentheses.

- Abraham Lincoln was the 16th president of the United States. (Consult biographies, social studies books, encyclopedias, and similar sources.)

- Earth revolves around the Sun. (Research in encyclopedias or astronomy books; ask knowledgeable people.)

- Dogs walk on four legs. (See for yourself.)

Opinions are statements that cannot be proved true. There is no objective evidence you can consult to check the truthfulness of an opinion. Unlike facts, opinions express personal beliefs or judgments. Opinions reveal how someone feels about a subject, not the facts about that subject. You might agree or disagree with someone's opinion, but you cannot prove it right or wrong.

Look at the following opinions. The reasons these statements are classified as opinions appear in parentheses.

- Abraham Lincoln was born to be a president. (You cannot prove this by referring to birth records. There is no evidence to support this belief.)

- Earth is the only planet in our solar system where intelligent life exists. (There is no proof of this. It may be proved true some day, but for now it is just an educated guess—not a fact.)

- The dog is a human's best friend. (This is not a fact; your best friend might not be a dog.)

As you read, be aware that facts and opinions are often mixed together. Both are useful to you as a reader. But to evaluate what you read and to read intelligently, you need to know the difference between the two.

Keeping Events in Order

Sequence, or chronological order, is the order of events in a story or article or the order of steps in a process. Paying attention to the sequence of events or steps will help you follow what is happening, predict what might happen next, and make sense of a passage.

To make the sequence as clear as possible, writers often use signal words to help the reader get a more exact idea of when things happen. Following is a list of frequently used signal words and phrases:

until	first
next	then
before	after
finally	later
when	while
during	now
at the end	by the time
as soon as	in the beginning

Signal words and phrases are also useful when a writer chooses to relate details or events out of sequence. You need to pay careful attention to determine the correct chronological order.

Making Correct Inferences

Much of what you read *suggests* more than it *says*. Writers often do not state ideas directly in a text. They can't. Think of the time and space it would take to state every idea. And think of how boring that would be! Instead, writers leave it to you, the reader, to fill in the information they leave out—to make inferences. You do this by combining clues in the story or article with knowledge from your own experience.

You make many inferences every day. Suppose, for example, that you are visiting a friend's house for the first time. You see a bag of kitty litter. You infer (make an inference) that the family has a cat. Another day you overhear a conversation. You catch the names of two actors and the words *scene, dialogue,* and *directing.* You infer that the people are discussing a movie or play.

In these situations and others like them, you infer unstated information from what you observe or read. Readers must make inferences in order to understand text.

Be careful about the inferences you make. One set of facts may suggest several inferences. Some of these inferences could be faulty. A correct inference must be supported by evidence.

Remember that bag of kitty litter that caused you to infer that your friend has a cat? That could be a faulty inference. Perhaps your friend's family uses the kitty litter on their icy sidewalks to create traction. To be sure your inference is correct, you need more evidence.

Understanding Main Ideas

The main idea is the most important idea in a paragraph or passage—the idea that provides purpose and direction. The rest of the selection explains, develops, or supports the main idea. Without a main idea, there would be only a collection of unconnected thoughts.

In the following paragraph, the main idea is printed in italics. As you read, observe how the other sentences develop or explain the main idea.

Typhoon Chris hit with full fury today on the central coast of Japan. Heavy rain from the storm flooded the area. High waves carried many homes into the sea. People now fear that the heavy rains will cause mudslides in the central part of the country. The number of people killed by the storm may climb past the 200 mark by Saturday.

In this paragraph, the main-idea statement appears first. It is followed by sentences that explain, support, or give details. Sometimes the main idea appears at the end of a paragraph. Writers often put the main idea at the end of a paragraph when their purpose is to persuade or convince. Readers may be more open to a new idea if the reasons for it are presented first.

As you read the following paragraph, think about the overall impact of the supporting ideas. Their purpose is to convince the reader that the main idea in the last sentence should be accepted.

Last week there was a head-on collision at Huntington and Canton streets. Just a month ago a pedestrian was struck there. Fortunately, she was only slightly injured. In the past year, there have been more accidents there than at any other corner in the city. In fact, nearly 10 percent of all accidents in the city occur at the corner. This intersection is very dangerous, and a traffic signal should be installed there before a life is lost.

The details in the paragraph progress from least important to most important. They achieve their full effect in the main idea statement at the end.

In many cases, the main idea is not expressed in a single sentence. The reader is called upon to interpret all of the ideas expressed in the paragraph and to decide upon a main idea. Read the following paragraph.

> The American author Jack London was once a pupil at the Cole Grammar School in Oakland, California. Each morning the class sang a song. When the teacher noticed that Jack wouldn't sing, she sent him to the principal. He returned to class with a note. The note said that Jack could be excused from singing with the class if he would write an essay every morning.

In this paragraph, the reader has to interpret the individual ideas and to decide on a main idea. This main idea seems reasonable: Jack London's career as a writer began with a punishment in grammar school.

Understanding the concept of the main idea and knowing how to find it is important. Transferring that understanding to your reading and study is also important.

Working Through a Lesson

Part A

1. **Preview the article.** Locate the timed selection in Part A of the lesson that you are going to read. Wait for your teacher's signal to preview. You will have 20 seconds for previewing. Follow the previewing steps described on page 2.

2. **Read the article.** When your teacher gives you the signal, begin reading. Read carefully so that you will be able to answer questions about what you have read. When you finish reading, look at the board and note your reading time. Write this time at the bottom of the page on the line labeled Reading Time.

3. **Complete the exercises.** Answer the 10 questions that follow the article. There are 5 fact questions and 5 idea questions. Choose the best answer to each question and put an X in that box.

4. **Correct your work.** Use the Answer Key at the back of the book to check your answers. Circle any wrong answer and put an X in the box you should have marked. Record the number of correct answers on the appropriate line at the end of the lesson.

Part B

1. **Preview and read the passage.** Use the same techniques you

used to read Part A. Think about what you are reading.

2. **Complete the exercises.** Instructions are given for answering each category of question. There are 15 responses for you to record.

3. **Correct your work.** Use the Answer Key at the back of the book. Circle any wrong answer and write the correct letter or number next to it. Record the number of correct answers on the appropriate line at the end of the lesson.

Plotting Your Progress

1. **Find your reading rate.** Turn to the Reading Rate graph on page 116. Put an X at the point where the vertical line that represents the lesson intersects your reading time, shown along the left-hand side. The right-hand side of the graph will reveal your words-per-minute reading speed.

2. **Find your comprehension score.** Add your scores for Part A and Part B to determine your total number of correct answers. Turn to the Comprehension Score graph on page 117. Put an X at the point where the vertical line that represents your lesson intersects your total correct answers, shown along the left-hand side. The right-hand side of the graph will show the percentage of questions you answered correctly.

3. **Complete the Comprehension Skills Profile.** Turn to page 118. Record your incorrect answers for the Part B exercises. The five Part B skills are listed along the bottom. There are five columns of boxes, one column for each question. For every incorrect answer, put an X in a box for that skill.

To get the most benefit from these lessons, you need to take charge of your own progress in improving your reading speed and comprehension. Studying these graphs will help you to see whether your reading rate is increasing and to determine what skills you need to work on. Your teacher will also review the graphs to check your progress.

About the Series

Timed Readings Plus in Science includes 10 books at reading levels 4–13, with one book at each level. Book One contains material at a fourth-grade reading level; Book Two at a fifth-grade level, and so on. The readability level is determined by the Fry Readability Scale and is not to be confused with grade or age level. The books are designed for use with students at middle-school level and above.

The purposes of the series are as follows:

- to provide systematic, structured reading practice that helps students improve their reading rate and comprehension skills

- to give students practice in reading and understanding informational articles in the content area of science

- to give students experience in reading various text types—informational, expository, narrative, and prescriptive

- to prepare students for taking standardized tests that include timed reading passages in various content areas

- to provide materials with a wide range of reading levels so that students can continue to practice and improve their reading rate and comprehension skills

Because the books are designed for use with students at designated reading levels rather than in a particular grade, the science topics in this series are not correlated to any grade-level curriculum. Most standardized tests require students to read and comprehend science passages. This series provides an opportunity for students to become familiar with the particular requirements of reading science. For example, the vocabulary in a science article is important. Students need to know certain words in order to understand the concepts and the information.

Each book in the series contains 25 two-part lessons. Part A focuses on improving reading rate. This section of the lesson consists of a 400-word timed informational article on a science topic followed by two multiple-choice exercises. Recalling Facts includes five fact questions; Understanding Ideas includes five critical-thinking questions.

Part B concentrates on building mastery in critical areas of comprehension. This section consists of a nontimed passage—the "plus" passage—followed by five exercises that address five major comprehension skills. The passage varies in length; its subject matter relates to the content of the timed selection.

Timed Reading and Comprehension

Timed reading is the best-known method of improving reading speed. There is no point in someone's reading at an accelerated speed if the person does not understand what she or he is reading. Nothing is more important than comprehension in reading. The main purpose of reading is to gain knowledge and insight, to understand the information that the writer and the text are communicating.

Few students will be able to read a passage once and answer all of the questions correctly. A score of 70 to 80 percent correct is normal. If the student gets 90 or 100 percent correct, he or she is either reading too slowly, or the material is at too low a reading level. A comprehension or critical thinking score of less than 70 percent indicates a need for improvement.

One method of improving comprehension and critical-thinking skills is for the student to go back and study each incorrect answer. First, the student should reread the question carefully. It is surprising how many students get the wrong answer simply because they have not read the question carefully. Then the student should look back in the passage to find the place where the question is answered, reread that part of the passage, and think about how to arrive at the correct answer. It is important to be able to recognize a correct answer when it is embedded in the text. Teacher guidance or class discussion will help the student find an answer.

Speed Versus Comprehension

It is not unusual for comprehension scores to decline as reading rate increases during the early weeks of timed readings. If this happens, students should attempt to level off their speed—but not lower it—and concentrate more on comprehension. Usually, if students maintain the higher speed and concentrate on comprehension, scores will gradually improve and within a week or two be back up to normal levels of 70 to 80 percent.

It is important to achieve a proper balance between speed and comprehension. An inefficient reader typically reads everything at one speed, usually slowly. Some poor readers, however, read rapidly but without satisfactory comprehension. It is important to achieve a balance between speed and comprehension. The practice that this series provides enables students to increase their reading speed while maintaining normal levels of comprehension.

Getting Started

As a rule, the passages in a book designed to improve reading speed should be relatively easy. The student should not have much difficulty with the vocabulary or the subject matter. Don't worry about the passages being too easy; students should see how quickly and efficiently they can read a passage.

Begin by assigning students to a level. A student should start with a book that is one level below his or her current reading level. If a student's reading level is not known, a suitable starting point would be one or two levels below the student's present grade in school.

Introduce students to the contents and format of the book they are using. Examine the book to see how it is organized. Talk about the parts of each lesson. Discuss the purpose of timed reading and the use of the progress graphs at the back of the book.

Timing the Reading

One suggestion for timing the reading is to have all students begin reading the selection at the same time. After one minute, write on the board the time that has elapsed and begin updating it at 10-second intervals (1:00, 1:10, 1:20, etc.). Another option is to have individual students time themselves with a stopwatch.

Teaching a Lesson

Part A

1. Give students the signal to begin previewing the lesson. Allow 20 seconds, then discuss special science terms or vocabulary that students found.

2. Use one of the methods described above to time students as they read the passage. (Include the 20-second preview time as part of the first minute.) Tell students to write down the last time shown on the board or the stopwatch when they finish reading. Have them record the time in the designated space after the passage.

3. Next, have students complete the exercises in Part A. Work with them to check their answers, using the Answer Key that begins on page 114. Have them circle incorrect answers, mark the correct answers, and then record the numbers of correct answers for Part A on the appropriate line at the end of the lesson. Correct responses to eight or more questions indicate satisfactory comprehension and recall.

Part B

1. Have students read the Part B passage and complete the exercises that follow it. Directions are provided with each exercise. Correct responses require deliberation and discrimination.

2. Work with students to check their answers. Then discuss the answers with them and have them record the number of correct answers for Part B at the end of the lesson.

Have students study the correct answers to the questions they answered incorrectly. It is important that they understand why a particular answer is correct or incorrect.

Have them reread relevant parts of a passage to clarify an answer. An effective cooperative activity is to have students work in pairs to discuss their answers, explain why they chose the answers they did, and try to resolve differences.

Monitoring Progress

Have students find their total correct answers for the lesson and record their reading time and scores on the graphs on pages 116 and 117. Then have them complete the Comprehension Skills Profile on page 118. For each incorrect response to a question in Part B, students should mark an X in the box above each question type.

The legend on the Reading Rate graph automatically converts reading times to words-per-minute rates. The Comprehension Score graph automatically converts the raw scores to percentages.

These graphs provide a visual record of a student's progress. This record gives the student and you an opportunity to evaluate the student's progress and to determine the types of exercises and skills he or she needs to concentrate on.

Diagnosis and Evaluation

The following are typical reading rates.

Slow Reader—150 Words Per Minute

Average Reader—250 Words Per Minute

Fast Reader—350 Words Per Minute

A student who consistently reads at an average or above-average rate (with satisfactory comprehension) is ready to advance to the next book in the series.

A column of Xs in the Comprehension Skills Profile indicates a specific comprehension weakness. Using the profile, you can assess trends in student performance and suggest remedial work if necessary.

Rain Forests: Tropical and Temperate

Whether temperate or tropical, all rain forests share certain characteristics. They are dense, they receive a lot of rain each year, and they contain a wide variety of plant and animal life. The differences between tropical and temperate rain forests include location, temperature, and most common life forms.

Tropical rain forests have existed for millions of years in areas near the equator where the climate is warm and moist. These forests are found in Latin America, West Africa, Australia, the Pacific islands, southern India, and Southeast Asia.

Temperate rain forests are far less widespread than tropical rain forests and have not been around for nearly as long. Most temperate rain forests occur along the northwest coast of North America. Some temperate rain forests can also be found in South America, Europe, and Asia. These forests exist only in places where continental mountain ranges stretch along the coast, not far from the ocean. When clouds travel in from the sea, they "bump into" the mountains. This prevents the clouds from moving farther inland. Instead, the mountains force the clouds up into cooler air, where water vapor condenses and falls to earth as rain. All this rain falls along the coast, drenching the temperate forest that grows there.

Temperate rain forests receive between 200 and 500 centimeters (80 and 200 inches) of rain a year; a tropical forest may receive as much as 1,000 centimeters (400 inches). Rain forests are the only kinds of forests that maintain an average temperature. For a temperate forest, this might be 15° Celsius (about 60° Fahrenheit); for a tropical forest, 25° Celsius (about 80° Fahrenheit).

All rain forests teem with life, harboring millions of species of plants and animals, but each type of forest has its own characteristic inhabitants. A mammal such as a brown bear might live in a temperate forest; a howler monkey is a mammal that might live in a tropical forest. Similarly, though both types of forest are rich with plant life, the Douglas fir might be found in a temperate rain forest, whereas the cocoa tree may live in a tropical one.

Warmth, humidity, and an abundance of rainfall are ideal conditions for the proliferation of life, which is why rain forests contain such a wide diversity of species. Though more than one million rain-forest species have been described, scientists believe there are millions more that haven't been found or identified yet.

Reading Time _____

Recalling Facts

1. A cocoa tree would be found in
   - ❑ a. a temperate rain forest.
   - ❑ b. a tropical rain forest.
   - ❑ c. neither a temperate nor a tropical rain forest.

2. Tropical rain forests are located
   - ❑ a. mostly within North America.
   - ❑ b. near an ocean.
   - ❑ c. near the equator.

3. The conditions found in rain forests have led to great
   - ❑ a. species diversity.
   - ❑ b. flooding.
   - ❑ c. cloud cover.

4. Temperate rain forests are formed in coastal regions bordered by
   - ❑ a. beaches.
   - ❑ b. deserts.
   - ❑ c. mountains.

5. The temperatures in both temperate and tropical rain forests
   - ❑ a. are about 25°C year round.
   - ❑ b. vary a great deal with the seasons.
   - ❑ c. mostly remain constant.

Understanding Ideas

6. A temperate rain forest is most likely to receive _____ of rainfall as a tropical rain forest.
   - ❑ a. more than twice the amount
   - ❑ b. half the amount
   - ❑ c. about the same amount

7. In which of the following places would a person be closest to a rain forest?
   - ❑ a. Dayton, Ohio
   - ❑ b. Seattle, Washington
   - ❑ c. Paterson, New Jersey

8. From the information found in the article, one can assume that
   - ❑ a. life forms not yet discovered might still be found in rain forests.
   - ❑ b. all of the life forms in the rain forest have been categorized and identified.
   - ❑ c. rain forests have exhausted their reserves and cannot support any other life forms.

9. To determine whether a rain forest is temperate or tropical, one would most want to know
   - ❑ a. its distribution of rainfall throughout the year.
   - ❑ b. the kind of precipitation it receives.
   - ❑ c. its location in relation to the equator.

10. If the temperature in a tropical rain forest decreased by 20 degrees, one could assume that life in the rain forest would be
   - ❑ a. greatly affected.
   - ❑ b. somewhat affected.
   - ❑ c. not affected at all.

Manaus: City in the Amazon Rain Forest

Manaus is a city in Brazil that was founded by the Portuguese in 1669. It is the capital of Amazonas, a tropical forest state in northwest Brazil spanning 1.5 million square kilometers (932,100 square miles) of the Amazon rain forest. Manaus is located on the Negro River, near the point where it meets the Amazon River.

Manaus, a central port town, was vital to the growth of the Amazon River as a shipping route. Manaus's port system is unique in Brazil. Because the Negro River is prone to heavy flooding, Manaus's port has a system of mooring lines built on rafts.

Located in the heart of the Amazon rain forest, Manaus is rich in natural resources. With growing demand for automobile tires in the early 1900s, rubber was Manaus's chief export and source of income. In fact, Manaus was one of the leading exporters of rubber to the world. In recent decades, however, car tires have been made out of synthetic rubber, so natural rubber has lost its value as an export for Manaus. Some local people, though, still make their living as rubber tappers.

Currently, Brazil nuts are one of Manaus's main exports. The city also exports large amounts of rosewood oil and jute, a fiber gathered from rain forest trees for use in making cord. Ecotourism and scientific missions also bring much-needed income to the Manaus region.

1. Recognizing Words in Context

Find the word *prone* in the passage. One definition below is closest to the meaning of that word. One definition has the opposite or nearly opposite meaning. The remaining definition has a completely different meaning. Label the definitions C for *closest*, O for *opposite or nearly opposite*, and D for *different*.

_____ a. needing to add

_____ b. likely to experience

_____ c. protected against

2. Distinguishing Fact from Opinion

Two of the statements below present *facts*, which can be proved correct. The other statement is an *opinion*, which expresses someone's thoughts or beliefs. Label the statements F for *fact* and O for *opinion*.

_____ a. Manaus was founded in 1669.

_____ b. Without the auto market, Manaus would never have been prosperous.

_____ c. Rubber is still an export for Manaus.

3. Keeping Events in Order

Label the events below 1, 2, and 3 to show the order in which the events happened.

_____ a. Manaus began exporting rubber.

_____ b. Synthetic rubber was invented.

_____ c. The auto market began to grow.

4. Making Correct Inferences

Two of the statements below are correct *inferences,* or reasonable guesses. They are based on information in the passage. The other statement is an incorrect, or faulty, inference. Label the statements C for *correct* inference and F for *faulty* inference.

_____ a. Once synthetic rubber was invented, Manaus had nothing left to export.

_____ b. Manaus's location as a port town has contributed to its economic success.

_____ c. The plants of the rain forest help provide Manaus with material for export.

5. Understanding Main Ideas

One of the statements below expresses the main idea of the passage. One statement is too general, or too broad. The other explains only part of the passage; it is too narrow. Label the statements M for *main idea,* B for *too broad,* and N for *too narrow.*

_____ a. Manaus is rich in history and natural resources.

_____ b. Manaus exports Brazil nuts.

_____ c. Manaus is in Amazonas.

Correct Answers, Part A _____

Correct Answers, Part B _____

Total Correct Answers _____

The Science of Navigational Sailing

Advances in the science of navigational sailing led to European sailors' exploration of the world. Prior to the 15th century, European explorers did not venture far from their continent. The reason was that sailing ships had only crude methods of navigating, based on the observation of wind patterns, currents, and the flight of seabirds. Once scientists and mathematicians developed more accurate navigational data and equipment, however, sailors became less fearful of the open ocean. Only then did they venture far beyond familiar coastal waters to explore new lands.

The science of celestial navigation developed out of astronomy. European astronomers had noticed that all the stars in the night sky appeared to rotate around one particular star. Located in the northern part of the sky, this star was called the North Star, or Polaris. Viewed from anywhere north of the equator, the star appears at a point in the sky that is approximately above the North Pole.

The discovery of the importance of the North Star was vital because explorers were finally able to determine their latitude, or position north of the equator. Latitude is expressed as an angle, measured in degrees. Navigators sailing north of the equator could calculate latitude by finding the angle between the horizon and the North Star. At the equator, or 0° latitude, the North Star appears directly on the horizon. South of the equator, sailors had to determine their latitude from the position of the noontime sun, a more difficult calculation.

It took navigators much longer to find a way to accurately calculate longitude, the east-west location of an object. In 1675 the British government established an observatory at Greenwich, England, to compile precise astronomical data for use by sailors. Scientists had already determined that longitude could be calculated by comparing the time of day from two different locations. Each hour of difference between the two times was equivalent to a difference of 15° in longitude between the two locations. It was decided that the time of day in Greenwich would be used as a standard for calculating longitude. Sailors could calculate the time of day at their ship's location by observing the position of the moon. All they needed was a highly accurate clock that could keep track of Greenwich time. When such a clock was developed in the 1760s, sailors could precisely calculate both latitude and longitude. This constituted a revolution in the science of navigation.

Reading Time _____

Recalling Facts

1. The science of celestial navigation grew out of
   - ❏ a. geography.
   - ❏ b. astronomy.
   - ❏ c. botany.

2. The North Star is also known as
   - ❏ a. Polaris.
   - ❏ b. Vega.
   - ❏ c. the sun.

3. Distance north or south of the equator is known as
   - ❏ a. latitude.
   - ❏ b. longitude.
   - ❏ c. altitude.

4. For each hour of difference between Greenwich time and local time, the difference in longitude is
   - ❏ a. 15°.
   - ❏ b. 30°.
   - ❏ c. 45°.

5. Portuguese explorers sailing south of the equator had to determine their latitude from the position of the
   - ❏ a. moon.
   - ❏ b. North Star.
   - ❏ c. noontime sun.

Understanding Ideas

6. From the information in the article, one can conclude that Christopher Columbus would have had the greatest difficulty calculating
   - ❏ a. latitude.
   - ❏ b. longitude.
   - ❏ c. the position of the moon.

7. In addition to accurate clocks, what other invention would have greatly benefited European sailors?
   - ❏ a. a high-magnification microscope
   - ❏ b. a highly accurate compass
   - ❏ c. a printing press

8. From the information in the article, one can infer that the meaning of the word *celestial* has to do with
   - ❏ a. stars.
   - ❏ b. ships.
   - ❏ c. Portugal.

9. One can conclude that European exploration was heavily influenced by
   - ❏ a. advances in navigational science.
   - ❏ b. the political situation in 15th-century Europe.
   - ❏ c. the wind patterns and currents of the South Atlantic Ocean.

10. It can be inferred from the article that a ship traveling diagonally relative to the equator experiences a change in its
    - ❏ a. latitude and longitude.
    - ❏ b. latitude only.
    - ❏ c. longitude only.

The Astrolabe

One of the oldest tools used to help determine an object's position on Earth is the astrolabe. Developed as early as the fourth or third century B.C., the astrolabe guided early explorers and helped create an interest in the science of celestial navigation.

The first astrolabes were flat wood or metal disks marked with the 360 degrees of circumference. These marks could be used to measure the angles from the horizon to the various stars and planets, as well as the moon. Sailors could compare these readings with detailed numerical charts to find their ship's location. Although quite useful, these early tools had their limits.

As sailing methods improved, so did astrolabes. In the 15th century more advanced astrolabes were developed, featuring a movable plate engraved with a map of the night sky. After setting the instrument to the correct date and time and aligning it with the sky overhead, sailors could determine not only their latitude but also when sunrise and sunset would occur. This increase in precision allowed sailors to travel to distant places without the fear of getting lost. European sailors traveled all over the world. An even more sophisticated instrument called the sextant supplanted the astrolabe in the 1700s.

1. **Recognizing Words in Context**

   Find the word *supplanted* in the passage. One definition below is closest to the meaning of that word. One definition has the opposite or nearly opposite meaning. The remaining definition has a completely different meaning. Label the definitions C for *closest,* O for *opposite or nearly opposite,* and D for *different.*

   _____ a. replaced

   _____ b. found the position of

   _____ c. was replaced by

2. **Distinguishing Fact from Opinion**

   Two of the statements below present *facts,* which can be proved correct. The other statement is an *opinion,* which expresses someone's thoughts or beliefs. Label the statements F for *fact* and O for *opinion.*

   _____ a. An astrolabe is an instrument used to measure an object's position on Earth.

   _____ b. In the 1400s, navigating a ship was difficult.

   _____ c. More advanced astrolabes were developed in the 15th century.

3. Keeping Events in Order

Label the events below 1, 2, and 3 to show the order in which the events happened.

_____ a. Sailors in the 1800s used sextants for navigation.

_____ b. New astrolabes allowed sailors to predict when sunrise and sunset would occur.

_____ c. Ancient people developed the first astrolabes.

4. Making Correct Inferences

Two of the statements below are correct *inferences*, or reasonable guesses. They are based on information in the passage. The other statement is an incorrect, or faulty, inference. Label the statements C for *correct* inference and F for *faulty* inference.

_____ a. The effectiveness of astrolabes has varied over time.

_____ b. A wise ship captain in the 1400s could navigate his way around the world by using only an astrolabe.

_____ c. A knowledge of astronomy was helpful to early navigators.

5. Understanding Main Ideas

One of the statements below expresses the main idea of the passage. One statement is too general, or too broad. The other explains only part of the passage; it is too narrow. Label the statements M for *main idea*, B for *too broad*, and N for *too narrow*.

_____ a. Astrolabes improved during the 15th century.

_____ b. The astrolabe played an important role in the early history of ship navigation.

_____ c. Astrolabes and sextants have played important roles in navigation.

Correct Answers, Part A _____

Correct Answers, Part B _____

Total Correct Answers _____

Sculpture on a Grand Scale

For thousand of years, artists have been carving rock. Sometimes their sculptures have consisted of small statues, and at other times they have sculpted entire buildings. Mount Rushmore and the Crazy Horse Memorial are two examples of rock sculpture on an even larger scale. Both of these wonders are carved out of mountains in the Black Hills of South Dakota.

In 1927, the sculptor Gutzon Borglum began work on Mount Rushmore. The Mount Rushmore sculpture represents the faces of four of the most admired U.S. presidents: George Washington, Thomas Jefferson, Abraham Lincoln, and Theodore Roosevelt. Borglum carved the monument into the side of a mountain of granite. The granite found in the Black Hills is among the oldest rock in the world.

The size of the monument is awe inspiring. The heads are proportional to bodies that would stand 140 meters (465 feet) tall. The faces look down from an elevation of about 1700 meters (5500 feet) above sea level. Borglum wanted the sculpture to be huge to signify the emergence of the United States as a world power.

Borglum employed almost 400 miners during his work on the project. They performed such jobs as constructing roads, measuring areas of granite, sharpening pneumatic drill bits, and using dynamite to blast away rock. Borglum worked on the monument from 1927 until his death in 1941. His son worked for seven months after his death to complete the faces. The monument is actually unfinished. Borglum intended for the sculpture to extend down to the presidents' waists.

The Crazy Horse Memorial, which is being created to honor the Sioux chief Crazy Horse, is located on a mountain of pink granite in the Black Hills. Korczak Ziolkowski, who worked for a short time for Borglum on Mount Rushmore, was invited by the Lakota Sioux to carve this gigantic tribute. Inspired by Crazy Horse's words "My lands are where my dead lie buried," Ziolkowski wrote a 21-line poem which will eventually be included as part of the monument.

Although Ziolkowski at first intended for the Crazy Horse Memorial to be only 30 meters (100 feet) high, he chose instead to carve the whole mountain. Although Ziolkowski died in 1982, his family continues the work. When finished, the sculpture will be 172 meters (563 feet) high and 195 meters (641 feet) long. It is even taller than Mount Rushmore, which is just 28 kilometers (17 miles) away.

Reading Time _____

Recalling Facts

1. Mount Rushmore commemorates U.S.
   - ❑ a. pioneers.
   - ❑ b. soldiers.
   - ❑ c. presidents.

2. Mount Rushmore was sculpted by
   - ❑ a. Borglum.
   - ❑ b. Ziolkowski.
   - ❑ c. Moore.

3. Both the Crazy Horse Memorial and Mount Rushmore are carved from
   - ❑ a. basalt.
   - ❑ b. marble.
   - ❑ c. granite.

4. Crazy Horse was a chief of the
   _____.
   - ❑ a. Apache
   - ❑ b. Sioux
   - ❑ c. Cheyenne

5. The region of South Dakota in which both monuments are located is called
   - ❑ a. the Great Divide.
   - ❑ b. the Rocky Mountains.
   - ❑ c. the Black Hills.

Understanding Ideas

6. The article suggests that granite
   - ❑ a. can be carved quickly.
   - ❑ b. is formed from minerals deposited by rivers.
   - ❑ c. is a strong rock that does not wear away quickly.

7. One can conclude that Borglum wanted to create Mount Rushmore to
   - ❑ a. provide Americans with a long-lasting monument to U.S. history.
   - ❑ b. prove that he was a greater sculptor than Ziolkowski.
   - ❑ c. attract tourists to South Dakota.

8. A word that would seem to describe Korczak Ziolkowski is
   - ❑ a. determined.
   - ❑ b. weak.
   - ❑ c. impatient.

9. From the article, one can assume that Ziolkowski
   - ❑ a. met Chief Crazy Horse at the 1876 Battle of the Little Bighorn.
   - ❑ b. was related to Gutzon Borglum.
   - ❑ c. had great respect for Chief Crazy Horse.

10. Which of the following is *not* true of both Mount Rushmore and the Crazy Horse monuments?
    - ❑ a. Both were created to honor people.
    - ❑ b. Both are made of sedimentary rock.
    - ❑ c. Both are ambitious works of sculpture.

Elemental Expression

Through the centuries, sculpture has been a consistently popular art form.
People of all ages enjoy sculpting sand castles at the seashore. Even the
youngest child is able to hold a lump of clay and create a form. The organic
connection to the earth that mud, sand, and stone provide has spiritual
qualities for some people, and it provides a fundamental basis for self-
expression. Stone is one of the most popular materials for sculpting.

Isamu Noguchi, a Japanese-American sculptor, considered stone to be a
healing medium for his sculpture. To him, stone was a symbol for nature
and the planet Earth. He used granite and basalt to create large, simple art
forms that are admired around the world. Granite and basalt are igneous;
that is, they are formed from the magma of volcanoes. Noguchi often left
the natural surfaces of his pieces untouched, allowing the beauty of the
stone to become part of the art.

Noguchi began his career in the 1930s. His intent was to make sculpture
accessible to the general public. Many of his sculptures take the form of
large pieces for public places, such as parks. His first public sculpture,
History Mexico, is a brick relief sculpture 22 meters (72 feet) long in
Mexico City. Relief sculpture is constructed along a flat surface. Noguchi
also created fountains and landscape gardens.

1. **Recognizing Words in Context**

   Find the word *organic* in the passage.
   One definition below is closest to the
   meaning of that word. One definition
   has the opposite or nearly opposite
   meaning. The remaining definition
   has a completely different meaning.
   Label the definitions C for *closest*, O
   for *opposite or nearly opposite*, and D
   for *different*.

   _____ a. natural

   _____ b. musical

   _____ c. artificial

2. **Distinguishing Fact from Opinion**

   Two of the statements below present
   facts, which can be proved correct.
   The other statement is an *opinion*,
   which expresses someone's thoughts
   or beliefs. Label the statements F for
   fact and O for *opinion*.

   _____ a. Noguchi was one of the
   finest sculptors of stone.

   _____ b. Noguchi often worked in
   granite.

   _____ c. Granite is an igneous rock.

3. **Keeping Events in Order**

Label the events below 1, 2, and 3 to show the order in which the events happened.

_____ a. Noguchi finished *History Mexico*.

_____ b. Noguchi was born.

_____ c. Noguchi began his career as a sculptor.

4. **Making Correct Inferences**

Two of the statements below are correct *inferences*, or reasonable guesses. They are based on information in the passage. The other statement is an incorrect, or faulty, inference. Label the statements C for *correct* inference and F for *faulty* inference.

_____ a. A stone sculpture may have a soothing effect on the viewer.

_____ b. Stone has a wide variety of uses in art.

_____ c. Noguchi created sculpture only for gardens and parks.

5. **Understanding Main Ideas**

One of the statements below expresses the main idea of the passage. One statement is too general, or too broad. The other explains only part of the passage; it is too narrow. Label the statements M for *main idea*, B for *too broad*, and N for *too narrow*.

_____ a. Sculptors have been working with rock for centuries.

_____ b. Isamu Noguchi was a sculptor who created many works from stone.

_____ c. Isamu Noguchi began his career in the 1930s.

Correct Answers, Part A _____

Correct Answers, Part B _____

Total Correct Answers _____

The Milky Way

Our solar system is part of the Milky Way galaxy, believed to have formed more than 16 billion years ago. Earth is approximately 27,000 light years from the center of the galaxy, and the edge of the galaxy is another 45,000 light years beyond Earth. A light year is the distance that light travels through space in one year. Astronomers think that the Milky Way formed from a large, spherical cloud of cold gas. This cloud rotated in space and collapsed upon itself. This process of collapsing, called condensing, is also the way numerous individual stars formed.

The Milky Way is one of many spiral galaxies. It consists of several regions and contains hundreds of billions of stars. The outer edge of the galaxy is called the galactic halo. It is composed of gas clouds, approximately 170 star clusters, and a few solitary stars. The galactic halo does not rotate in tandem with the rest of the galaxy, and it contains quite a bit of dark matter. Dark matter is a substance that cannot be seen and is not well understood; it is believed to account for the majority of the Milky Way's mass. The stars found in the galactic halo are called Population 2 stars and are at least 12 billion years old.

The region next to the galactic halo is known as the thick disk, a flat area of gas and stars that rotates slowly around the galaxy's center. The next region, an even flatter disk of stars called the thin disk, rotates more rapidly around the center. The extreme disk is located closer still to the galaxy's center. Here the stars are young, ranging from 1 billion to 10 billion years old. The extreme disk rotates even more rapidly than the thin disk does.

Astronomers have found strong evidence of an enormous black hole at the center of the Milky Way. The black hole is called Sagittarius A. It is surrounded by a spherical cluster of stars called the central bulge. Here many new stars are forming while others are dying or exploding.

The oldest stars in the galactic halo provide evidence that the Milky Way has grown over the eons, partly by swallowing smaller galaxies. The Milky Way itself is speeding toward the Andromeda galaxy at about 500,000 kilometers (310,000 miles) per hour. Astronomers believe that these two galaxies will coalesce, perhaps in about 2 billion years.

Reading Time _____

Recalling Facts

1. Our solar system is part of
   - ❑ a. Sagittarius A.
   - ❑ b. the Andromeda galaxy.
   - ❑ c. the Milky Way galaxy.

2. The Milky Way is a _____ galaxy.
   - ❑ a. linear
   - ❑ b. spiral
   - ❑ c. circular

3. Most of the mass of the Milky Way is contained in
   - ❑ a. dark matter.
   - ❑ b. gaseous clouds.
   - ❑ c. globular clusters.

4. The outer edge of the Milky Way galaxy is called the
   - ❑ a. solar system.
   - ❑ b. thick disk.
   - ❑ c. galactic halo.

5. The black hole in the center of the Milky Way galaxy is called
   - ❑ a. Population 2.
   - ❑ b. Sagittarius A.
   - ❑ c. Dark Matter.

Understanding Ideas

6. Compared with stars found on the outer edge of the Milky Way galaxy, stars found on the thin disk are likely
   - ❑ a. older.
   - ❑ b. younger.
   - ❑ c. the same age.

7. Which of the following is *not* a reasonable conclusion about the Milky Way?
   - ❑ a. There are other stars similar to our Sun in the galaxy.
   - ❑ b. The Milky Way is in a state of constant movement.
   - ❑ c. Scientists have a detailed understanding of all regions of the galaxy.

8. One can assume that in the distant future, the Milky Way galaxy will change
   - ❑ a. significantly.
   - ❑ b. not at all.
   - ❑ c. slightly.

9. Earth is closest to _____ of the Milky Way.
   - ❑ a. the center
   - ❑ b. the edge
   - ❑ c. the point halfway between the center and the edge

10. One can conclude from this article that astronomers _____ about how the Milky Way formed.
    - ❑ a. have an idea
    - ❑ b. have no idea
    - ❑ c. are worried

Globular star clusters consist of some of the oldest known stars in the galaxy. Most of them are 16 billion to 18 billion years old. The clusters are composed of the pristine gases that formed the galaxy. Astronomers can tell the age of globular clusters by the type of gases they contain.

When the Milky Way was formed, there were perhaps thousands of these clusters. Today, only about 200 remain, and conditions are no longer conducive to the creation of new clusters. The surviving globular clusters are older than anything found on Earth. Each cluster contains hundreds of thousands of stars. These stars move symmetrically around a common center of gravity, and the clusters themselves orbit the center of the galaxy. Some of the orbits take millions of years to complete. The orbits of these clusters help astronomers to calculate the amount of mass in the galaxy.

Harlow Shapley was the first scientist to describe globular star clusters. In 1918, he studied how the clusters were distributed in the galaxy. His estimates of the size of the galaxy, and the position of the Sun within it, were far more accurate than previous estimates. Helen Sawyer Hogg was another astronomer who dedicated her career to observing globular star clusters. She did important research on variable stars, which are stars that emit varying amounts of light.

1. **Recognizing Words in Context**

   Find the word *conducive* in the passage. One definition below is closest to the meaning of that word. One definition has the opposite or nearly opposite meaning. The remaining definition has a completely different meaning. Label the definitions C for *closest*, O for *opposite or nearly opposite*, and D for *different*.

   _____ a. magnetic

   _____ b. resistant

   _____ c. favorable

2. **Distinguishing Fact from Opinion**

   Two of the statements below present *facts*, which can be proved correct. The other statement is an *opinion*, which expresses someone's thoughts or beliefs. Label the statements F for *fact* and O for *opinion*.

   _____ a. Harlow Shapley was smarter than previous astronomers.

   _____ b. Globular star clusters are billions of years old.

   _____ c. Helen Sawyer Hogg studied variable stars.

3. **Keeping Events in Order**

Label the statements below 1, 2, and 3 to show the order in which the events happened.

_____ a. The Milky Way was formed.

_____ b. Globular star clusters stopped being formed.

_____ c. The youngest globular star cluster was formed.

4. **Making Correct Inferences**

Two of the statements below are correct *inferences,* or reasonable guesses. They are based on information in the passage. The other statement is an incorrect, or faulty, inference. Label the statements C for *correct* inference and F for *faulty* inference.

_____ a. Understanding globular star clusters will help us understand more about our galaxy.

_____ b. The number of globular star clusters will continue to slowly increase.

_____ c. Some of the material in the clusters is as old as the galaxy itself.

5. **Understanding Main Ideas**

One of the statements below expresses the main idea of the passage. One statement is too general, or too broad. The other explains only part of the passage; it is too narrow. Label the statements M for *main idea*, B for *too broad*, and N for *too narrow.*

_____ a. Stars provide information about the galaxy.

_____ b. The orbits of some star clusters last for millions of years.

_____ c. Globular star clusters provide clues about the age, formation, and size of the galaxy.

Correct Answers, Part A _____

Correct Answers, Part B _____

Total Correct Answers _____

Snow serves many purposes. Building snowpeople, making snow angels, and having snowball fights are ways that people have fun with snow. However, snow also provides great benefits to the earth as well. Snow and snow cover are important to ecosystems in many ways.

When snow melts at the start of spring, it becomes a major source of water. The water that snowfall eventually produces is an important contributor to supplies of drinking and irrigation water. Snow also has a reflective property. New snowfall possesses 80 to 90 percent reflectivity. This property, combined with snow's insulating qualities, works to alter the exchange of energy between the surface of the planet and the atmosphere. Air temperatures are lower by 5 to 10 Celsius degrees (9 to 18 Fahrenheit degrees) when there is snow cover. When there is extensive snow cover, cold air can travel longer distances before it warms up. This produces winters that are colder than usual and can delay the planting of crops.

The insulating property of snow results from the air between snow crystals. Light, fluffy snow is a better insulator than icy, packed snow. Snow cover reduces the depth that frost penetrates into the soil. Frozen soil can kill the roots of some beneficial plants. Animals are instinctively aware of snow's insulating properties. Hibernating animals, such as ground squirrels, can obtain a few degrees of extra warmth by finding a spot under the snow. When an animal hibernates, it dramatically reduces its basic energy consumption, living off its fat reserves. By taking cover under the snow, these animals stay a few degrees warmer and can better conserve their reserves of body fat, making it easier for them survive the winter. Although many animals lie dormant in winter, some animals, such as weasels, voles, and mice, find shelter in the snow layer and remain active year-round.

Humans also use snow to keep warm. A quinzee—a temporary structure used by northern native peoples—is made by piling snow in a large mound, allowing it to "set," and then scooping out a small chamber to use as shelter. Igloos also are popular structures among people in the Arctic. Hard-packed snow is cut into blocks that are then fitted together. Body heat helps keep the inside of the igloo warm. Snow can also be piled against an existing shelter, such as a house or tent, to afford additional insulation to that shelter.

Reading Time _____

Recalling Facts

1. One of snow's greatest benefits is its
   - ❏ a. temperature.
   - ❏ b. appearance.
   - ❏ c. insulating property.

2. Snow cover holds heat in the ground because snow crystals trap
   - ❏ a. air.
   - ❏ b. water.
   - ❏ c. dirt.

3. Melting snow provides a major source of
   - ❏ a. carbon dioxide.
   - ❏ b. air.
   - ❏ c. water.

4. During the winter, a hibernating animal lives off of
   - ❏ a. whatever food it can find.
   - ❏ b. its fat reserves.
   - ❏ c. underground water supplies.

5. A quinzee is a
   - ❏ a. temporary structure made of snow.
   - ❏ b. hibernating animal.
   - ❏ c. layer of soil that does not freeze.

Understanding Ideas

6. If a region experienced significantly less snowfall than usual, the most probable outcome would be that
   - ❏ a. water pollution would increase.
   - ❏ b. more people would move into the area.
   - ❏ c. agriculture would suffer.

7. The most likely result of heavy snowfall would be
   - ❏ a. additional water in reservoirs.
   - ❏ b. a decrease in flooding.
   - ❏ c. a record harvest.

8. Why might gardeners put a layer of dead leaves on their gardens at the start of winter?
   - ❏ a. to prevent the soil from freezing and killing flower bulbs
   - ❏ b. to fertilize the soil in the middle of winter
   - ❏ c. to avoid the need to burn the leaves

9. Probably the most effective way to increase the temperature inside an igloo would be to
   - ❏ a. put warm clothing on the ground.
   - ❏ b. increase the number of people in the igloo.
   - ❏ c. light a candle.

10. In order to survive the winter, hibernating animals need to find a warm place to sleep and
    - ❏ a. eat an ample supply of food during the summer.
    - ❏ b. stay in constant motion during the summer.
    - ❏ c. keep their coats well groomed and healthy.

5 B   Surviving Blizzards

Although snow can be a beautiful part of winter, it can also be a powerful and deadly force. When caught outside in blizzards, people can become disoriented. They can even freeze to death.

If trapped in a storm, it's important to preserve as much body heat as possible. First, seek shelter. If necessary, dig a snow cave or try to build a shelter with rocks. Help conserve body heat with a blanket and extra clothing if they are available. When in a forest, insulate the body with evergreen boughs. Keep hands, head, and feet covered, and cover the mouth and nose with cloth.

The major cause of death in extreme cold is hypothermia. It dulls the brain, the organ most vital for survival. Hypothermia comes on in stages. Shivering is the first sign of stage one. Speech becomes slurred, and coordination suffers. After the body's temperature drops below 35° Celsius (95° Fahrenheit), stage two begins. Stage-two symptoms include muscular rigidity and increased irrationality. The victim is often the last one to know he or she is in danger. Be aware of the behavior of those nearby; their actions can signal a warning.

Local weather stations provide up-to-the-minute information about approaching storms. When traveling outdoors in cold weather, always have a first-aid kit, emergency supplies, extra clothes, and a radio close at hand.

1. **Recognizing Words in Context**

   Find the word *disoriented* in the passage. One definition below is closest to the meaning of that word. One definition has the opposite or nearly opposite meaning. The remaining definition has a completely different meaning. Label the definitions C for *closest*, O for *opposite or nearly opposite*, and D for *different*.

   _____ a. confused

   _____ b. alert

   _____ c. determined

2. **Distinguishing Fact from Opinion**

   Two of the statements below present *facts*, which can be proved correct. The other statement is an *opinion*, which expresses someone's thoughts or beliefs. Label the statements F for *fact* and O for *opinion*.

   _____ a. People who take part in winter sports are asking for trouble.

   _____ b. Local weather forecasts can provide information about storms.

   _____ c. Hypothermia is the major cause of death in extreme cold.

3. Keeping Events in Order

Label the statements below 1, 2, and 3 to show the order in which the events happen.

_____ a. A victim of hypothermia experiences muscle rigidity.

_____ b. A victim of hypothermia experiences slurred speech.

_____ c. A victim of hypothermia begins shivering.

4. Making Correct Inferences

Two of the statements below are correct *inferences,* or reasonable guesses. They are based on information in the passage. The other statement is an incorrect, or faulty, inference. Label the statements C for *correct* inference and F for *faulty* inference.

_____ a. Traveling in groups is safer than traveling alone in winter weather.

_____ b. Following all safety precautions will always keep a person safe in winter weather.

_____ c. Keeping the hands and feet covered can help prevent hypothermia.

5. Understanding Main Ideas

One of the statements below expresses the main idea of the passage. One statement is too general, or too broad. The other explains only part of the passage; it is too narrow. Label the statements M for *main idea,* B for *too broad,* and N for *too narrow.*

_____ a. Bad weather can kill people.

_____ b. Following safety precautions can help people stay safe when they are outside in winter weather.

_____ c. Keep a first-aid kit nearby when traveling in winter weather.

Correct Answers, Part A _____

Correct Answers, Part B _____

Total Correct Answers _____

Renewable Energy Sources

"Renewable energy" refers to energy that cannot be used up. Some of the most common types of renewable energy are solar, wind, geothermal, hydroelectric, and biomass energy. Geothermal energy comes from the heat deep beneath the ground. Hydroelectric energy comes from moving water. The Sun, Earth, wind, and water are considered infinite sources of energy. Biomass energy comes from plants and waste material that are continually resupplied.

Solar energy is derived from the Sun. The energy in sunlight can be captured by many types of solar collectors. They absorb light and convert it to heat. Solar energy has many uses. It can be used to heat water. It can also be used to cool homes and buildings. Solar power works best in regions where the sky is seldom overcast. Cloudy skies block some of the sunlight from reaching solar collectors.

Energy from the wind is captured by large turbines with propeller-like blades. Many turbines stand as high as 30 meters (100 feet). Wind turbines can supply electricity directly to buildings, or their electricity can be sent through power lines. Wind farms, which are areas with high concentrations of turbines, provide large amounts of wind energy. Some power companies distribute electricity created by wind turbines.

Geothermal energy is obtained from hot water and steam below ground. Underground volcanic activity heats groundwater to temperatures at or above the boiling point. The water and steam can be removed by drilling and used to heat homes. Several cities in Iceland rely on geothermal energy to heat their buildings. In the United States there are geothermal plants in northern California, Alaska, and Hawaii.

Hydroelectric power comes from flowing water. Hydroelectric power is the largest source of renewable energy in the United States. Nearly 10 percent of U.S. energy comes from water. Dams produce most hydroelectric power. Many dams have turbines; when water flows through the dam, the turbines spin and produce electricity in generators.

Biomass energy comes from organic matter that can be used to produce electricity, provide heat, and make fuel. Wood is the main source of biomass energy. Wood-burning stoves are used to heat homes in some parts of the world. Other sources of biomass energy include manure, the organic part of industrial waste, and waste products from logging operations. Biomass can be converted directly into liquid fuels such as ethanol and biodiesel. These fuels are then used to operate cars and planes.

Reading Time _____

Recalling Facts

1. Energy derived from sources that can't be used up is called
   - ❏ a. finite energy.
   - ❏ b. nuclear energy.
   - ❏ c. renewable energy.

2. Solar collectors convert the sun's rays into
   - ❏ a. heat.
   - ❏ b. hydroelectricity.
   - ❏ c. gasoline vapor.

3. Wind energy is captured by
   - ❏ a. turbines.
   - ❏ b. combustion engines.
   - ❏ c. solar collectors.

4. Hydroelectric power is derived from
   - ❏ a. wind.
   - ❏ b. heat.
   - ❏ c. water.

5. The main source of biomass energy is
   - ❏ a. an electromagnetic field.
   - ❏ b. wood.
   - ❏ c. coal.

Understanding Ideas

6. Which source of renewable energy would be available in all parts of the country?
   - ❏ a. geothermal wells
   - ❏ b. hydroelectric dams
   - ❏ c. biomass

7. From the information in the passage, one can conclude that turbines can be powered by
   - ❏ a. only wind.
   - ❏ b. both wind and water.
   - ❏ c. only water.

8. Which of the following energy sources would *not* be considered renewable?
   - ❏ a. coal
   - ❏ b. trees
   - ❏ c. rivers

9. Changes in _____ would most effectively decrease our use of energy in the future.
   - ❏ a. military equipment
   - ❏ b. manufacturing facilities
   - ❏ c. transportation methods

10. One hundred years from now, it is most likely that
    - ❏ a. people will be using energy from new sources.
    - ❏ b. people will no longer need energy sources.
    - ❏ c. all renewable resources will be depleted.

The Hoover Dam

One of the most impressive structures in the United States is the Hoover Dam. This dam supplies low-cost hydroelectric power to Arizona, Nevada, and California. Construction of the dam began in 1930. It was completed five years later. The dam was originally named Boulder Dam. It was renamed Hoover Dam in honor of Herbert Hoover, who had been involved with this project even before he became president of the United States. Before construction of the dam could start, Hoover had to help resolve a disagreement among seven western states about water allocation from the Colorado River basin.

The amount of concrete used to build the Hoover Dam would be enough to pave a street from San Francisco to New York. The dam is 220 meters (726 feet) high. At its base, it is 506 meters (1,660 feet) wide. Hoover Dam is designed to store 35 million liters (9.2 million gallons) of water in its reservoir, Lake Mead. This is about two years worth of average yearly river flow. Lake Mead is the largest reservoir in the United States. It extends 187 kilometers (115 miles) north of the Hoover Dam. The dam is one key part of a system that brings water to millions of people in the southwestern United States.

1. Recognizing Words in Context

Find the word *allocation* in the passage. One definition below is closest to the meaning of that word. One definition has the opposite or nearly opposite meaning. The remaining definition has a completely different meaning. Label the definitions C for *closest*, O for *opposite or nearly opposite*, and D for *different*.

_____ a. collection

_____ b. distribution

_____ c. position

2. Distinguishing Fact from Opinion

Two of the statements below present *facts*, which can be proved correct. The other statement is an *opinion*, which expresses someone's thoughts or beliefs. Label the statements F for *fact* and O for *opinion*.

_____ a. The Hoover Dam is an amazing piece of architecture.

_____ b. The Hoover Dam's reservoir is called Lake Mead.

_____ c. The Hoover Dam supplies low-cost power to Arizona, California, and Nevada.

3. Keeping Events in Order

Label the events below 1, 2, and 3 to show the order in which the events happened.

_____ a. Construction of the dam began.

_____ b. Boulder Dam was renamed Hoover Dam.

_____ c. Herbert Hoover resolved a water allocation dispute.

4. Making Correct Inferences

Two of the statements below are correct *inferences,* or reasonable guesses. They are based on information in the passage. The other statement is an incorrect, or faulty, inference. Label the statements C for *correct* inference and F for *faulty* inference.

_____ a. The Hoover Dam is important to people in the Southwest.

_____ b. The Hoover Dam is the only source of power in the Southwest.

_____ c. Building the Hoover Dam required a lot of planning.

5. Understanding Main Ideas

One of the statements below expresses the main idea of the passage. One statement is too general, or too broad. The other explains only part of the passage; it is too narrow. Label the statements M for *main idea,* B for *too broad,* and N for *too narrow.*

_____ a. The Hoover Dam is a large structure and major power producer.

_____ b. Dams can be used to create electricity.

_____ c. Lake Mead is the largest reservoir in the United States.

Correct Answers, Part A _____

Correct Answers, Part B _____

Total Correct Answers _____

Penicillin: The Wonder Drug

Penicillin has been called the first miracle drug. An antibiotic, penicillin has helped people to live healthier lives. An antibiotic is a substance that kills bacteria or prevents them from reproducing. Prior to the discovery of penicillin, many people died of common illnesses, such as infections, that are treatable today.

In 1929, Alexander Fleming, a Scottish scientist, became the first person to notice the potential value of penicillin. Fleming had been using petri dishes to grow bacteria, and he noticed that penicillium mold had started to grow on one of the dishes. He saw that no bacteria had grown in the area of the fungus. Although unable to identify what substance in the mold prevented the growth of bacteria, Fleming was able to provide data on the mold's power to kill and prevent the spread of germs.

In 1938, Howard Florey and Ernst Chain, building on Fleming's work, were able to separate the antibiotic substance, penicillin, from the penicillium mold and make it available for use in medicine. The three men later shared a Nobel Prize for the discovery of penicillin. During World War II, funding became available to do more research on the drug. By the time World War II ended, 650 billion units of the drug had been produced. In addition to the penicillin obtained from mold, some other types of penicillin have been created artificially in laboratories.

Penicillin works as an antibiotic because it interferes with the reproductive process of bacteria. Bacteria reproduce by dividing in two. To do this, they must create new cell walls between the separating halves. Penicillin stops these new cell walls from forming.

One problem with the effectiveness of penicillin has arisen. Over time, bacteria can become resistant to certain antibiotics. Scientists are constantly developing new types of antibiotics that work on bacteria that have developed resistance to other antibiotics.

Antibiotics do not work on viral illnesses, such as colds or influenza. A person who has a virus should not take an antibiotic. Not only will the antibiotic do nothing to harm the virus, it may destroy harmless bacteria and even the helpful bacteria that live in the intestines. An unnecessary antibiotic can also help harmful bacteria build resistance to the drug.

In the United States today, the number of deaths from bacterial infections has dropped by 95 percent since 1900. Much of this is the result of the discovery of penicillin.

Reading Time _____

Recalling Facts

1. Penicillin is a type of
   - ❏ a. infection.
   - ❏ b. antibiotic.
   - ❏ c. bacterium.

2. The antibiotic potential of penicillium mold was first noticed by
   - ❏ a. Howard Florey.
   - ❏ b. Ernst Chain.
   - ❏ c. Alexander Fleming.

3. Which of the following statements is *not* true?
   - ❏ a. Bacteria can build up resistance to antibiotics.
   - ❏ b. Antibiotics work on all diseases.
   - ❏ c. Some antibiotics are found in fungus.

4. Penicillin stops bacteria from reproducing by
   - ❏ a. preventing them from forming new cell walls.
   - ❏ b. killing their eggs.
   - ❏ c. disabling the feeding mechanism of male bacteria.

5. Antibiotics are effective against
   - ❏ a. colds.
   - ❏ b. bacterial infections.
   - ❏ c. influenza.

Understanding Ideas

6. The most likely reason for the increased funding for penicillin development during World War II is
   - ❏ a. soldiers were dying when their wounds became infected.
   - ❏ b. economic conditions were excellent worldwide.
   - ❏ c. soldiers benefited from taking antibiotics during training.

7. One of the greatest benefits of the discovery of penicillin is
   - ❏ a. fewer deaths from infections.
   - ❏ b. the discovery of related drugs for viral infections.
   - ❏ c. the destruction of all bacteria.

8. If people take antibiotics when they do not have a bacterial disease, it is likely that they will
   - ❏ a. be less likely to get colds.
   - ❏ b. disrupt the way their intestines work.
   - ❏ c. become less likely to get any type of infection.

9. One can conclude that
   - ❏ a. everyone responds to disease in the same way.
   - ❏ b. once we find a cure for a disease, it is no longer a threat to anybody.
   - ❏ c. diseases can change over time, requiring new drugs to treat them.

10. One can infer that Alexander Fleming first discovered the potential medical benefit of penicillium mold
   - ❏ a. through careful planning.
   - ❏ b. by accident.
   - ❏ c. by reading research.

Bacteria are single-celled organisms that provide many benefits. Pathogenic bacteria cause disease, but most bacteria are very helpful. Some bacteria live in intestines and aid in the digestion of food. Others break dead organisms down into basic chemical compounds that can be used by other organisms.

Bacteria also help make minerals in the soil available to plants for food. Plants depend on soil as a source of food and water. Countless numbers of helpful bacteria inhabit the soil, making it healthy for plants to grow. Plants need nitrogen to thrive. Some bacteria are able to absorb nitrogen from the air and convert it into forms that plants can use. By helping plants, bacteria help other life forms. All animals need plants for survival. Even animals that eat meat and no plants depend on plants: many of the animals they eat are plant eaters. In addition, plants produce much of the oxygen in the atmosphere.

Bacteria come in many shapes. Some are round, and some are spiral-shaped; others have long, whiplike tails. Bacteria are found everywhere and can live in all climates; they have even been found in boiling underground water near volcanoes.

Bacteria have been around for billions of years. One reason is that they multiply quickly. A single "parent" cell splits to form two "daughter" cells. Under favorable conditions, this can occur every 20 to 30 minutes.

1. **Recognizing Words in Context**

   Find the word *pathogenic* in the passage. One definition below is closest to the meaning of that word. One definition has the opposite or nearly opposite meaning. The remaining definition has a completely different meaning. Label the definitions C for *closest*, O for *opposite or nearly opposite*, and D for *different*.

   _____ a. harmful

   _____ b. helpful

   _____ c. movable

2. **Distinguishing Fact from Opinion**

   Two of the statements below present *facts*, which can be proved correct. The other statement is an *opinion*, which expresses someone's thoughts or beliefs. Label the statements F for *fact* and O for *opinion*.

   _____ a. Scientists have found that some bacteria can be helpful.

   _____ b. Bacteria do more harm than good.

   _____ c. Bacteria help break down decaying matter.

3. Keeping Events in Order

Label the statements below 1, 2, and 3 to show the order in which the events happen.

_____ a. The decomposed organism returns nutrients to the soil.

_____ b. An organism dies.

_____ c. Bacteria work to break down the organism.

4. Making Correct Inferences

Two of the statements below are correct *inferences*, or reasonable guesses. They are based on information in the passage. The other statement is an incorrect, or faulty, inference. Label the statements C for *correct* inference and F for *faulty* inference.

_____ a. If all bacteria were removed from the soil, plants would suffer.

_____ b. To lead healthy lives, people need bacteria.

_____ c. All bacteria have the potential to cause disease.

5. Understanding Main Ideas

One of the statements below expresses the main idea of the passage. One statement is too general, or too broad. The other explains only part of the passage; it is too narrow. Label the statements M for *main idea*, B for *too broad*, and N for *too narrow*.

_____ a. Some of the smallest living things are some of the most important.

_____ b. Bacteria can add nitrogen to soil.

_____ c. Bacteria are single-celled organisms that provide many benefits.

Correct Answers, Part A _____

Correct Answers, Part B _____

Total Correct Answers _____

Urban Sprawl

In the United States during the 20th century, there was a dramatic increase in the amount of land taken up by urban areas. Many people moved from farms and rural communities to cities and the towns that surround cities. In 1900, only 40 percent of the U.S. population lived in urban areas. By 1960, about 70 percent of the population was in urban areas. Since 1960, the most rapidly growing areas in the country have been the suburbs.

Along with increases in the populations of cities and suburbs has come the construction of many new homes, businesses, and streets. When such construction is rapid and not well planned, it can result in a condition known as urban sprawl. Some of the features of urban sprawl are large housing subdivisions, traffic jams, and block after block of malls and mini-malls.

Urban sprawl has an impact on the environment, as it causes a loss of what is called green space. For example, between 1982 and 1997, about 101,000 square kilometers (39,000 square miles) of rural lands were lost as they were developed into city and suburban properties. Urban sprawl has played a major role in the decline of natural habitats such as wetlands and woodlands. Because of this environmental impact, sprawl is sometimes referred to as habitat encroachment. This loss of habitat has resulted in the threat of extinction for some animal and plant species.

Some suburban growth resulted from people's moving out of large cities. As cars became less expensive and more easily maintained, driving soon became the norm. Companies began moving outside of cities to areas that had lower taxes and cheaper land. Many of their workers had cars and had no problem commuting to new locations. The workers also began to move to the suburbs as more jobs and better schools became available there. As the move to the perimeter of cities accelerated, urban sprawl began to set in.

One of the solutions to sprawl may lie in alternative transportation choices. Although many large cities have mass-transit systems, many of their suburban areas do not. The many people who live in one suburb and work in another often have no choice but to drive. The construction of special networks of buses and trains specifically for suburban areas would allow more people to avoid driving. This would cut down on the pollution from car exhaust and ease traffic jams.

Reading Time _____

Recalling Facts

1. Since 1900 the percentage of the population living in rural areas has
   - ❏ a. stayed about the same.
   - ❏ b. decreased.
   - ❏ c. increased.

2. One feature of urban sprawl is
   - ❏ a. large train systems.
   - ❏ b. large parks.
   - ❏ c. large subdivisions.

3. One of the biggest problems of urban sprawl is that
   - ❏ a. cars break down sooner.
   - ❏ b. fewer jobs are available.
   - ❏ c. animal habitat is lost.

4. Since 1960 the most rapidly growing areas have been
   - ❏ a. suburbs.
   - ❏ b. small towns.
   - ❏ c. large cities.

5. Improvements in _____ contributed most to urban sprawl.
   - ❏ a. factories
   - ❏ b. automobiles
   - ❏ c. shopping malls

Understanding Ideas

6. A major obstacle to combating urban sprawl would be
   - ❏ a. an increased number of buses.
   - ❏ b. continued growth in suburban areas.
   - ❏ c. fewer subdivisions.

7. A likely factor in people's moving from large cities to the suburbs would be
   - ❏ a. less expensive education.
   - ❏ b. better mass transit.
   - ❏ c. the fear of crime.

8. Which of the following is most likely to occur if urban sprawl continues unchecked?
   - ❏ a. It will take longer for people in the suburbs to drive to work.
   - ❏ b. Local governments will buy shopping malls and turn them into parks.
   - ❏ c. Most people will move from suburbs to large cities.

9. From the article, one could assume that more people would move back into large cities if there were more
   - ❏ a. affordable houses in neighborhoods with good schools.
   - ❏ b. office buildings with luxury apartments on top.
   - ❏ c. habitat for threatened species.

10. It has become increasingly difficult for families to earn a sufficient income on small farms. How might this affect urban sprawl?
    - ❏ a. It will have no effect.
    - ❏ b. It will decrease it.
    - ❏ c. It will increase it.

City living can often be fast paced and stressful. Large parks can provide a much-needed place for city dwellers to relax and spend time with family and friends. Such parks also help preserve the natural landscape while adding beauty to an otherwise drab urban environment.

Frederick Law Olmsted is known as the father of American landscape and architectural design. He spent much of his career designing urban parks that worked in harmony with the natural landscape, including part of Central Park in New York City. As much as possible, he tried to use forests, wetlands, and other natural elements in his designs.

One of the best known of Olmsted's works is a series of connected parks in Boston known as the Emerald Necklace. Work on this park system began in 1887. It is one of the oldest systems of connected parks in the nation. Olmsted had already designed two parks in Boston, the Arnold Arboretum and the Back Bay Fens. When he created the Emerald Necklace, he joined these two parks and designed several others.

Two prominent parts of the Emerald Necklace are Jamaica Pond and Franklin Park. Jamaica Pond was Boston's first drinking water reservoir. Today, it is a place for jogging, walking, and boating. Franklin Park is the largest section of the Emerald Necklace. It includes hiking trails, the Franklin Park Zoo, and a golf course.

1. **Recognizing Words in Context**

   Find the word *drab* in the passage. One definition below is closest to the meaning of that word. One definition has the opposite or nearly opposite meaning. The remaining definition has a completely different meaning. Label the definitions C for *closest,* O for *opposite or nearly opposite,* and D for *different.*

   _____ a. exciting

   _____ b. polluted

   _____ c. dull

2. **Distinguishing Fact from Opinion**

   Two of the statements below present *facts,* which can be proved correct. The other statement is an *opinion,* which expresses someone's thoughts or beliefs. Label the statements F for *fact* and O for *opinion.*

   _____ a. The Emerald Necklace is one of the most beautiful park systems in the country.

   _____ b. Olmsted designed arboretums.

   _____ c. The Emerald Necklace is located in Boston.

3. Keeping Events in Order

Label the statements below 1, 2, and 3 to show the order in which the events happened.

_____ a. Olmsted finished his design for the Emerald Necklace.

_____ b. Olmsted designed Arnold Arboretum.

_____ c. Workers completed the construction of Franklin Park.

4. Making Correct Inferences

Two of the statements below are correct *inferences,* or reasonable guesses. They are based on information in the passage. The other statement is an incorrect, or faulty, inference. Label the statements C for *correct* inference and F for *faulty* inference.

_____ a. Olmsted felt it was important to work with the natural landscape.

_____ b. The Emerald Necklace adds heavily to the Boston area.

_____ c. Without the Emerald Necklace, most people would not enjoy living in Boston.

5. Understanding Main Ideas

One of the statements below expresses the main idea of the passage. One statement is too general, or too broad. The other explains only part of the passage; it is too narrow. Label the statements M for *main idea,* B for *too broad,* and N for *too narrow.*

_____ a. The Emerald Necklace is a unique system of connected parks in Boston.

_____ b. Parks are a valued part of city life.

_____ c. Frederick Law Olmsted was a pioneer of landscape architecture.

Correct Answers, Part A _____

Correct Answers, Part B _____

Total Correct Answers _____

Sea Otters

Otters are mammals and are part of the weasel family, which means they are closely related to such animals as ferrets and minks. Otters are playful animals that possess natural curiosity and high levels of energy and intelligence. There are 13 known species in existence.

The sea otter is the only one of these 13 species that lives only in a saltwater environment. Sea otters can be found in the northern Pacific Ocean in coastal waters along Alaska, and in smaller numbers along Washington, California, and Russia.

Sea otters spend nearly all of their time in the water. They have keenly sensitive whiskers that help them to navigate through the ocean and to locate prey. They eat, sleep, and have babies in the water, preferring areas that contain kelp. Sea otters will frequently use thick bunches of kelp to hold themselves in place while they sleep. Adult sea otters must eat the equivalent of 25 percent of their body weight every day, as a huge amount of energy is needed to survive the ocean's intense cold. One of their favorite foods is abalone, a type of sea snail; they also eat clams and crab. They have learned to break open shellfish on rocks. Unlike most other members of the weasel family, sea otters like to live in groups.

Sea otter fur is the thickest fur in the world. Sea otters spend almost half of each day grooming their fur. The fur has two layers—a dense undercoat and a topcoat of longer guard hairs. The water-repellent topcoat protects the undercoat, which traps a layer of air next to the skin. This helps keep the sea otter dry and warm. Sea otters are the only marine mammals that do not have a layer of blubber. In the 18th century, otter fur became fashionable for coats, and by 1900 the sea otter had been hunted nearly to extinction, disappearing entirely from the coasts of Japan, Mexico, and Canada.

Conservation efforts have partially restored the sea otter population, but these and other animals that live in cold northern waters face a new threat in the form of oil spills from tankers and other ships. Because the sea otter doesn't have a thick layer of blubber, it relies on its fur to keep warm. If it swims into oily waters, the fur loses its insulating properties; the otter becomes chilled and may die.

Reading Time _____

Recalling Facts

1. Sea otters use rocks as
   - ❏ a. food.
   - ❏ b. weapons.
   - ❏ c. tools.

2. A favorite food of the otter is
   - ❏ a. kelp.
   - ❏ b. abalone.
   - ❏ c. seagull.

3. Which of the following statements is *not* true?
   - ❏ a. Otters spend much of their time grooming.
   - ❏ b. There are 13 known species of otters in existence.
   - ❏ c. Otters have thin fur.

4. Sea otters spend their time
   - ❏ a. mostly on land.
   - ❏ b. mostly in the water.
   - ❏ c. about equally on land and in water.

5. An otter's fur has
   - ❏ a. two layers.
   - ❏ b. one layer.
   - ❏ c. three layers.

Understanding Ideas

6. What is the most likely reason that the sea otter population has increased after nearly being wiped out?
   - ❏ a. Sea otters learned how to avoid hunters.
   - ❏ b. Sea otters moved to areas where there were no hunters.
   - ❏ c. The hunting of sea otters was made illegal.

7. One can assume that the sea otter population in 1700 was _____ the sea otter population today.
   - ❏ a. greater than
   - ❏ b. less than
   - ❏ c. the same as

8. Navigating with its whiskers, the sea otter has a highly developed sense of
   - ❏ a. hearing.
   - ❏ b. touch.
   - ❏ c. smell.

9. Which of the following would be most likely to happen?
   - ❏ a. A person sees a single sea otter off the coast of California.
   - ❏ b. A person sees six or seven sea otters off the coast of Alaska.
   - ❏ c. A person sees two or three sea otters off the coast of Japan.

10. One can assume that otters are most closely related to
    - ❏ a. badgers.
    - ❏ b. dolphins.
    - ❏ c. seals.

Smart Creatures

When anthropologists study the development of primitive human civilizations, one of the ways they determine a civilization's level of advancement is by looking at the type of tools that the people used. A tool can be defined as an object used as an extension of the body. Tool use is not limited to humankind. Some species of animals have thrived thanks to their adaptation of tools as a means of survival.

Primates are the most well-known tool users in the animal kingdom, but a few other kinds of animals also have developed tool-using capabilities. For example, when the woodpecker finch of the Galapagos Islands has trouble removing an insect or insect larva from a hole in a cactus or tree limb, it uses a cactus spine or twig to remove the insect. As the bird eats, it keeps the tool under its feet so it can reuse it for the next meal. The Egyptian vulture uses a rock to break open its favorite meal—ostrich eggs. Sometimes a vulture will search for a rock for a distance of up to 45 meters (50 yards), leaving the egg unattended.

Chimpanzees are able to construct tools from grass or twigs. They use these tools to extract termites from holes. Animals do not use tools just for getting food. Horses and elephants will sometimes hold a stick in their mouth or trunk to use as a backscratcher.

1. **Recognizing Words in Context**

Find the word *extension* in the passage. One definition below is closest to the meaning of that word. One definition has the opposite or nearly opposite meaning. The remaining definition has a completely different meaning. Label the definitions C for *closest*, O for *opposite or nearly opposite*, and D for *different*.

_____ a. reduction

_____ b. lengthening

_____ c. irritation

2. **Distinguishing Fact from Opinion**

Two of the statements below present *facts*, which can be proved correct. The other statement is an *opinion*, which expresses someone's thoughts or beliefs. Label the statements F for *fact* and O for *opinion*.

_____ a. Some animals use tools to obtain food.

_____ b. Animals that use tools are nearly as smart as humans are.

_____ c. Some animals use tools to scratch their backs.

3. Keeping Events in Order

Label the statements below 1, 2, and 3 to show the order in which the events happen.

_____ a. A woodpecker finch finds a cactus spine.

_____ b. A woodpecker finch pries the larva out of the hole.

_____ c. A woodpecker finch has trouble removing an insect larva from a hole in a cactus.

4. Making Correct Inferences

Two of the statements below are correct *inferences*, or reasonable guesses. They are based on information in the passage. The other statement is an incorrect, or faulty, inference. Label the statements C for *correct* inference and F for *faulty* inference.

_____ a. Tool use may have developed from a need to obtain food.

_____ b. In order for tool use to develop, an animal must have a way to grasp a tool.

_____ c. All animals are capable of using tools.

5. Understanding Main Ideas

One of the statements below expresses the main idea of the passage. One statement is too general, or too broad. The other explains only part of the passage; it is too narrow. Label the statements M for *main idea*, B for *too broad*, and N for *too narrow*.

_____ a. Some species of animals have learned to use tools.

_____ b. Scientists study similarities in behavior between human and animals.

_____ c. Egyptian vultures use rocks as tools.

Correct Answers, Part A _____

Correct Answers, Part B _____

Total Correct Answers _____

Two Kinds of Forests

Temperate deciduous forests and coniferous forests are two distinct types of biomes, or ecological systems. Humans benefit greatly from these forests, which generate oxygen and provide wood.

Temperate deciduous forests are found in the eastern United States, southeastern Canada, most of Europe, parts of China and Japan, and southern South America. Deciduous trees lose their leaves in the fall. Temperate deciduous forests receive 75 to 150 centimeters (30 to 60 inches) of precipitation per year. Temperatures range from about –30°C (–22°F) to 30°C (86°F). This biome can support a wide range of life forms; among the most common animals are squirrels, owls, and pigeons.

Temperate deciduous forests are characterized by five main strata, or layers. The highest layer is called the tree stratum. Trees found in this stratum include maples and beeches. The next layer is known as the small tree stratum; young trees and shorter tree species, such as dogwood, can be found here. The next layer is the shrub stratum, which consists of such plants as azaleas and huckleberries. Next is the herb stratum, which is home to very short plants. The layer nearest the ground is called the ground stratum—lichens and mosses live here.

Coniferous forests grow in the colder regions of the United States, Canada, Europe, and Asia. The trees in coniferous forests produce their seeds inside cone-shaped structures, such as pinecones. This type of forest—sometimes called the boreal forest—generally receives 30 to 90 centimeters (12 to 35 inches) of rainfall each year. The average summer temperature is about 10°C (50°C). Animals that have adapted well to cold climates, such as moose and woodland caribou, live in this forest.

The coniferous forest usually has three layers. The top layer is the canopy; it helps insulate lower layers from wind and temperature extremes. Canopy trees include Douglas fir, spruce, and jack pine. The middle layer is the shrub layer. Some species here are dogwood and honeysuckle. The layer closest to the ground is the ground layer. Mosses and herbs live here.

The needles that grow on some coniferous trees contain acid. As they fall to the earth and decompose, they leave behind a black, acidic layer called peat. When it rains, the acid in the peat seeps into the soil. This destroys nutrients needed by tree roots. Fungi that live in the trees' roots help offset the effects of the acid by producing minerals and nutrients.

Reading Time _____

Recalling Facts

1. One characteristic of deciduous forests is
   - ❑ a. high altitude.
   - ❑ b. five layers of plant life.
   - ❑ c. proximity to the ocean.

2. The second-lowest layer in a deciduous forest is the
   - ❑ a. ground layer.
   - ❑ b. shrub layer.
   - ❑ c. herb layer.

3. Coniferous trees produce _____ inside cone-shaped structures.
   - ❑ a. seeds
   - ❑ b. berries
   - ❑ c. needles

4. The needles of some coniferous trees are
   - ❑ a. alkaline.
   - ❑ b. acidic.
   - ❑ c. infectious.

5. _____ are found in the ground layer of both types of forests.
   - ❑ a. Azaleas
   - ❑ b. Huckleberries
   - ❑ c. Mosses

Understanding Ideas

6. Compared with deciduous forests, coniferous forests experience
   - ❑ a. shorter winters.
   - ❑ b. more rainfall.
   - ❑ c. more difficult growing conditions.

7. Which type of plant would you be most likely to find in the shrub layer of a temperate deciduous forest?
   - ❑ a. an elm tree
   - ❑ b. a blueberry bush
   - ❑ c. a wildflower

8. From the article, one can assume that mammals living in coniferous forests most likely
   - ❑ a. have thick coats of fur or hair.
   - ❑ b. are often nocturnal.
   - ❑ c. are most active in winter.

9. Plants growing on the ground layer of a temperate deciduous forest most likely need
   - ❑ a. a great deal of rain.
   - ❑ b. very little sunlight.
   - ❑ c. warm temperatures all year.

10. From the information in the article, one can infer that jack pine trees would grow best in
    - ❑ a. Canada.
    - ❑ b. Japan.
    - ❑ c. central Europe.

The Colorful Deaths of Leaves

The beautiful leaves that appear in autumn are part of a chemical process that deciduous trees undergo each year. Leaves from deciduous trees contain chlorophyll, a chemical that contains a green pigment. Chlorophyll not only gives leaves their green color but also absorbs energy from light and helps turn it into food for trees. As temperatures cool at the start of autumn, the tree's production of chlorophyll slows down and finally stops. The other leaf pigments that have been hidden by the chlorophyll are now revealed. Autumn leaves range in color from yellow to deep red because the leaves of different trees contain different kinds of pigments.

When leaves grow in the spring, they contain the structures that will cause them to fall in autumn. A layer of cells called the abscission layer is produced at the base of each leaf. During the summer, tiny tubes that pass through this layer bring water to the leaf and food to the tree. As autumn approaches, the cells swell and form a corklike seal that eventually cuts off the flow of water and food between the leaf and tree. As the seal forms, cells in the top of the abscission layer begin to disintegrate. This creates a tear line at the base of the leaf, and soon the dead leaf floats to the ground.

1. **Recognizing Words in Context**

   Find the word *deciduous* in the passage. One definition below is closest to the meaning of that word. One definition has the opposite or nearly opposite meaning. The remaining definition has a completely different meaning. Label the definitions C for *closest*, O for *opposite or nearly opposite*, and D for *different*.

   _____ a. attaching to

   _____ b. growing out

   _____ c. falling off

2. **Distinguishing Fact from Opinion**

   Two of the statements below present *facts*, which can be proved correct. The other statement is an *opinion*, which expresses someone's thoughts or beliefs. Label the statements F for *fact* and O for *opinion*.

   _____ a. Autumn is the prettiest time of the year.

   _____ b. Leaves contain chlorophyll.

   _____ c. Leaves begin to change color as temperatures fall.

3. Keeping Events in Order

Label the statements below 1, 2, and 3 to show the order in which the events happen.

_____ a. Summer comes to an end.

_____ b. Leaves on a tree turn yellow and orange.

_____ c. A tree begins to produce less chlorophyll.

4. Making Correct Inferences

Two of the statements below are correct *inferences,* or reasonable guesses. They are based on information in the passage. The other statement is an incorrect, or faulty, inference. Label the statements C for *correct* inference and F for *faulty* inference.

_____ a. The less chlorophyll present in the leaves, the more different colors will be visible.

_____ b. Trees with leaves that don't change color are not healthy.

_____ c. If temperatures stayed warm throughout the year, leaves would not change color.

5. Understanding Main Ideas

One of the statements below expresses the main idea of the passage. One statement is too general, or too broad. The other explains only part of the passage; it is too narrow. Label the statements M for *main idea,* B for *too broad,* and N for *too narrow.*

_____ a. Temperature affects the way plants grow.

_____ b. A chemical process accompanies the death of a leaf.

_____ c. Some leaves contain red pigments.

Correct Answers, Part A _____

Correct Answers, Part B _____

Total Correct Answers _____

11 A Desert Biomes

One-fifth of Earth's land is desert. Most deserts average less than 25 centimeters (10 inches) of rain per year. What rainfall there is usually occurs in short, heavy bursts and is followed by long periods of dry weather. Plants and animals that live in the desert have developed ways of adapting to the dryness and the often extreme temperatures.

The terrain and the atmosphere help shape the desert biome. Some deserts have formed near mountain ranges, because air loses moisture as it travels up and over mountains. Wind is another factor in the formation of deserts. Wind increases the rate at which water evaporates, and so wind can dry out soil.

Scientists disagree about what conditions are required for an area to be classified as a desert. Some believe that there are four different desert biomes: hot and dry, semi-arid, coastal, and cold. These categories are based on climate variations. Different kinds of life thrive in each type of desert.

Hot and dry deserts have year-round warm temperatures, frequently exceeding 38°C (100°F) during the daytime. The air is so dry that sometimes rain evaporates before it hits the ground. Most of the animals found here are nocturnal because the air is cooler at night, making it easier for them to move about and find food. Most plants are low to the ground and often have a thick outer layer to help retain water. Yucca, ocotillo, and prickly pear cacti are examples of plants found in this type of desert.

The semi-arid desert has more clearly defined seasons than the hot and dry desert. Plants here often have spines. These spines partially shade the surface of the plant, which helps it to retain water. Their spiny texture also provides protection. Examples of these plants are the creosote bush and the brush sage. Snakes live in this biome because they rarely drink water, obtaining their moisture from the prey they capture.

Coastal deserts are found in moderately cool to warm areas such as Chile where the soil is fairly porous with good drainage. Examples of coastal desert plants are the saltbush and rice grass. Animals include coyotes and toads.

Cold deserts have cold winters with some snowfall. Rainfall occurs frequently in winter and occasionally in the summer. These deserts are found in the Antarctic and Greenland. Plants are deciduous with spiny leaves. Birds are the most common animals.

Reading Time _____

Recalling Facts

1. A coastal desert can be found in
   - ❑ a. Chile.
   - ❑ b. Greenland.
   - ❑ c. Antarctica.

2. One characteristic of the desert biome is
   - ❑ a. dead trees.
   - ❑ b. winter snow.
   - ❑ c. a dry climate.

3. _____ sometimes contribute to the formation of deserts.
   - ❑ a. Humans
   - ❑ b. Mountains
   - ❑ c. Animals

4. Precipitation in the desert usually comes from
   - ❑ a. frequent light rain during spring.
   - ❑ b. brief rainstorms.
   - ❑ c. occasional snowfall.

5. An animal found in the semi-arid desert is the
   - ❑ a. snake.
   - ❑ b. bear.
   - ❑ c. deer.

Understanding Ideas

6. Which of the following statements is *not* true?
   - ❑ a. Cacti have been able to adapt to harsh desert conditions.
   - ❑ b. All types of deserts have the same seasons.
   - ❑ c. Deserts typically have limited rainfall through the course of a year.

7. If a person were lost in a desert, he or she could most probably get water from
   - ❑ a. cacti or other plants.
   - ❑ b. a nearby stream.
   - ❑ c. the air.

8. Plants that survive well in the desert most likely
   - ❑ a. do not require water.
   - ❑ b. retain water well.
   - ❑ c. retain water poorly.

9. From the article, one can conclude that
   - ❑ a. wind conditions are similar in all types of deserts.
   - ❑ b. deserts are typically located near streams.
   - ❑ c. life forms have found ways to adapt to harsh desert conditions.

10. An animal that makes its home in a hot and dry desert most likely
    - ❑ a. sleeps at night.
    - ❑ b. sleeps during the day.
    - ❑ c. requires a great deal of water.

The Saguaro Cactus

The saguaro cactus has a tall stem that averages 50 centimeters (20 inches) in diameter and is marked by long vertical grooves. When the cactus reaches middle age—about 75 years old—the stem often will grow several arms, which are long branches that curve upward. The waxy skin is covered with spines that can be as long as 5 centimeters (2 inches). Beautiful white flowers bloom at the ends of the arms during May and June. The cactus produces an egg-shaped green fruit that for centuries was an important food source for Native Americans. A saguaro can grow to a height of 15 meters (50 feet) and can weigh 900 kilograms (2,000 pounds).

In spite of their spines and thick skins, saguaro cacti serve as homes for several animals, including the Gila woodpecker. These birds peck holes in the cacti and build nests there. The woodpeckers are thoughtful guests—they do not make their holes after it has rained. If they did, they would hinder the process by which the cacti store water, and the cacti would die.

Each year the woodpeckers make new holes and abandon the previous ones. Insects, lizards, and elf owls make their homes in the abandoned holes. Among other guests are red-tailed hawks and Harris hawks, which build twig nests on the arms of the cacti.

1. **Recognizing Words in Context**

   Find the word *hinder* in the passage. One definition below is closest to the meaning of that word. One definition has the opposite or nearly opposite meaning. The remaining definition has a completely different meaning. Label the definitions C for *closest*, O for *opposite or nearly opposite*, and D for *different*.

   _____ a. assist

   _____ b. disrupt

   _____ c. leak

2. **Distinguishing Fact from Opinion**

   Two of the statements below present *facts*, which can be proved correct. The other statement is an *opinion*, which expresses someone's thoughts or beliefs. Label the statements F for *fact* and O for *opinion*.

   _____ a. Saguaros are home to several creatures.

   _____ b. Saguaros have a towering, majestic appearance.

   _____ c. Saguaros have sharp spines and green fruit.

3. Keeping Events in Order

Label the statements below 1, 2, and 3 to show the order in which the events happen.

_____ a. A Gila woodpecker drills a hole in a saguaro.

_____ b. Woodpecker chicks hatch in a saguaro.

_____ c. An elf owl moves into the abandoned hole.

4. Making Correct Inferences

Two of the statements below are correct *inferences,* or reasonable guesses. They are based on information in the passage. The other statement is an incorrect, or faulty, inference. Label the statements C for *correct* inference and F for *faulty* inference.

_____ a. Most saguaros have woodpecker holes.

_____ b. Saguaros are important to the desert ecosystem.

_____ c. Hawks build nests in the desert because some rodents live there.

5. Understanding Main Ideas

One of the statements below expresses the main idea of the passage. One statement is too general, or too broad. The other explains only part of the passage; it is too narrow. Label the statements M for *main idea,* B for *too broad, and* N for *too narrow.*

_____ a. The saguaro is a large cactus that serves as a home for animals.

_____ b. Cacti are desert plants.

_____ c. The red-tailed hawk eats lizards and snakes.

Correct Answers, Part A _____

Correct Answers, Part B _____

Total Correct Answers _____

The Artist and Light

Painters use their unique qualities of perception to create visually stimulating images, whether realistic or abstract. The way in which Vincent van Gogh portrayed a starry sky or Claude Monet created a landscape resulted in part from the way each of their minds responded to information conveyed by their eyes. Similarly, viewers of art use their eyes and minds to interpret paintings, forming their own ideas and opinions. Understanding the mechanics of vision is a starting point for understanding how art is created and appreciated.

Sight is a complex sense. The process of seeing begins when light rays pass through the lens at the front of the eye. The lens focuses the light to form an inverted image on the retina, the back surface of the eyeball. The retina contains two different kinds of light-sensitive cells called rods and cones. More than 100 million rods and cones cover the retina. These rods and cones convert light into neural, or nerve, impulses. The neural impulses travel to the brain, which converts them to a mental image.

Light is a form of energy that has wavelike properties. The color of an object is determined by the wavelength of the light that the object reflects. Although there are just seven base colors, the human eye is capable of detecting up to 10 million shades of color.

In an attempt to understand more about how vision works, the psychologist G. T. Buswell examined people's eyes while they viewed works of art. He was able to show that a person's gaze will follow the most distinctive line, whether straight or curved, in a work of art. In his experiment, Buswell used *The Great Wave Off Kanagawa,* a 19th-century woodblock print by the Japanese artist Hokusai. Buswell found that eyes spent the most consecutive moments following the curve of the wave. These results revealed that the eye and brain do not work like copying machines. Rather, they choose selectively on the basis of interest and intelligence what to focus on.

Scientists are trying to understand the psychological connection between vision and emotional responses. They have shown that the color yellow or red can raise a person's blood pressure. Shades of blue, on the other hand, have been shown to lower blood pressure. Therefore, a painter can create a certain mood by emphasizing certain colors. Likewise, creators of advertisements can use colors to manipulate the emotions of consumers.

Reading Time _____

Recalling Facts

1. A painting by Vincent van Gogh portrays _____
   - ❑ a. the Mona Lisa.
   - ❑ b. his mother in a rocking chair.
   - ❑ c. a starry night.

2. Light-sensitive cells found on the retina are called rods and
   - ❑ a. cubes.
   - ❑ b. cones.
   - ❑ c. sticks.

3. The colors that people see result from the _____ of light.
   - ❑ a. wavelength
   - ❑ b. particle size
   - ❑ c. brightness

4. A color that has been shown to lower blood pressure is
   - ❑ a. red.
   - ❑ b. yellow.
   - ❑ c. blue.

5. The brain receives information from the eyes in the form of
   - ❑ a. sonic waves.
   - ❑ b. neural impulses.
   - ❑ c. patterned vibrations.

Understanding Ideas

6. The article suggests that visual perception is
   - ❑ a. the same for each person.
   - ❑ b. a characteristic unique to artists.
   - ❑ c. unique to each person.

7. From the article, one can conclude that the eye would be most likely to focus on which part of a painting of a moving train?
   - ❑ a. the train tracks
   - ❑ b. thin, wispy clouds in the sky
   - ❑ c. grass beside the tracks

8. From the research by G. T. Buswell, one can conclude that a person looking at a painting tends to
   - ❑ a. concentrate on the painting as a whole.
   - ❑ b. focus on one part of the painting.
   - ❑ c. form opinions based on how realistic the painting is.

9. From the article, one can conclude that yellow light and red light have
   - ❑ a. the same wavelength.
   - ❑ b. different wavelengths.
   - ❑ c. no wavelengths.

10. From the article, you can infer that people who lead stressful lives might want to consider painting their bedroom
    - ❑ a. light blue.
    - ❑ b. red.
    - ❑ c. bright yellow.

Theatrical Lighting and Design

A person who designs the lighting for a play can create magical effects by employing different types of lamps. There are three types of lamps that lighting designers use most often: fresnels, pars, and floods. The fresnel spotlight has a soft-edged beam. Fresnels are useful for general lighting and for creating areas of color. A par lamp creates an intense, focused beam of light. It is very harsh and can be used to simulate bright sunlight and headlights, or it can be used as a narrow spotlight. Flood lamps, also known as floods, are used to illuminate a large area, such as a backdrop—the scenery at the back of the stage. A flood's beam can't be directed, so it is not useful for lighting smaller, more specific areas.

Lighting designers can use lamps to affect the way the audience perceives the actors. Backlighting can create a halo effect around an actor's head and shoulders. This helps to separate the actor from the background without creating shadows on her or his face. A silhouette effect is achieved by lighting only the background. This is a dramatic effect often used to create mystery and intrigue. Top lighting, also called downlighting, does not allow the audience to see an actor's eyes. Bottom lighting, also called uplighting, creates an eerie, unnatural effect.

1. **Recognizing Words in Context**

    Find the word *simulate* in the passage. One definition below is closest to the meaning of that word. One definition has the opposite or nearly opposite meaning. The remaining definition has a completely different meaning. Label the definitions C for *closest*, O for *opposite or nearly opposite*, and D for *different*.

    _____ a. mimic

    _____ b. originate

    _____ c. simplify

2. **Distinguishing Fact from Opinion**

    Two of the statements below present *facts*, which can be proved correct. The other statement is an *opinion*, which expresses someone's thoughts or beliefs. Label the statements F for *fact* and O for *opinion*.

    _____ a. Uplighting creates the scariest effect.

    _____ b. Flood lamps light large areas.

    _____ c. Three main types of lamps are used by lighting designers.

3. **Keeping Events in Order**

Label the statements below 1, 2, and 3 to show the order in which the events happen.

_____ a. The director consults with the lighting designer.

_____ b. The director wants to create an eerie atmosphere.

_____ c. The lighting designer uses uplighting.

4. **Making Correct Inferences**

Two of the statements below are correct *inferences*, or reasonable guesses. They are based on information in the passage. The other statement is an incorrect, or faulty, inference. Label the statements C for *correct* inference and F for *faulty* inference.

_____ a. All stage performances rely heavily on lighting effects.

_____ b. Lighting effects can help to create a mood for a performance.

_____ c. Pars can be used for scenes in which the action takes place outdoors during daytime hours.

5. **Understanding Main Ideas**

One of the statements below expresses the main idea of the passage. One statement is too general, or too broad. The other explains only part of the passage; it is too narrow. Label the statements M for *main idea*, B for *too broad*, and N for *too narrow*.

_____ a. Lighting and sound are important parts of theatrical productions.

_____ b. Lighting designers use many effects to achieve different moods in a performance.

_____ c. A fresnel is useful for general lighting.

Correct Answers, Part A _____

Correct Answers, Part B _____

Total Correct Answers _____

13 A Amphibians

The word *amphibian* means "both kinds of life." Amphibians are unusual in that they live both on the land and in the water. There are more than 4,000 species of amphibians in the world. The continental United States is home to about 230 species of amphibians. Of these, 90 are frog and toad species, and 140 are salamander species. People living near water are likely to see amphibians at some point.

Amphibians are ectothermic, or cold-blooded, which means their internal body temperature is the same as that of their surroundings. When a frog suns itself on a rock, it is trying to keep warm. Unlike humans, amphibians cannot increase their temperatures by moving about or by shivering, and they cannot stay cool by sweating. They need to move to different environments to change their body temperatures. They may move into the sun when they are cold or into the shade or underground when they are hot. Amphibians that live in places with harsh winters or hot summers become inactive when temperatures are extreme.

Most amphibians have four limbs and bodies covered with moist, smooth skin. Generally, amphibians' lives have two stages. Amphibians hatch from eggs laid in the water, beginning their existence as larvae that use gills to obtain oxygen. An example of such a larva is the tadpole. As the larvae grow into adults, they develop lungs and become able to breathe on land. Many adult amphibians also breathe through their skins, which must remain moist so that they can process oxygen properly. Adults shed their skins from time to time.

Amphibians are carnivorous, which means they eat other animals. Among their favorite foods are insects, spiders, worms, and snails. Amphibians function as important parts of food webs. They help control populations of insects, small mammals, reptiles, and other amphibians. They also serve as food for large fish, snakes, and birds. These feeding relationships help to ensure a proper balance in the ecosystem.

Amphibians also help humans by serving as bio-indicators. Because amphibians live on land and in the water, they are excellent yardsticks of many different environmental factors that humans may not be aware of. Amphibians' skin is permeable, which means that substances pass through it easily. As a result, amphibians are more sensitive to toxins than people are. So, for example, if biologists notice that frogs have suddenly disappeared from an area, they know there may be a pollution problem.

Reading Time _____

Recalling Facts

1. Amphibians live
   - ❏ a. only on land.
   - ❏ b. only in the water.
   - ❏ c. on land and in the water.

2. The word *amphibian* means
   - ❏ a. both kinds of life.
   - ❏ b. reptile.
   - ❏ c. dinosaur.

3. Most amphibians are born
   - ❏ a. underground.
   - ❏ b. in the water.
   - ❏ c. in the grass.

4. Amphibians eat
   - ❏ a. insects.
   - ❏ b. moss.
   - ❏ c. leaves.

5. Amphibians can breathe through their
   - ❏ a. ears.
   - ❏ b. feet.
   - ❏ c. skin.

Understanding Ideas

6. When an amphibian is cold, it is most likely to
   - ❏ a. shiver to keep warm.
   - ❏ b. move to a warmer place.
   - ❏ c. shed its skin.

7. One could conclude from the article that amphibians
   - ❏ a. include snakes and lizards.
   - ❏ b. are found mainly in the continental United States.
   - ❏ c. have adapted to many environments.

8. If the amphibian population declined considerably, one might assume that the insect population would
   - ❏ a. decrease.
   - ❏ b. increase.
   - ❏ c. remain the same.

9. Unlike adult amphibians, amphibian larvae
   - ❏ a. are able to shed their skins.
   - ❏ b. cannot breathe oxygen on land.
   - ❏ c. can live both on land and in the water.

10. The continued use of amphibians as bio-indicators should help people to
   - ❏ a. grow crops more effectively.
   - ❏ b. process oxygen more efficiently.
   - ❏ c. prevent dangerous environmental problems from becoming more serious.

Frog Food

The frog has had a long time to develop its unique method of consuming insects. The first frog appeared on Earth during the Jurassic Period—almost 190 million years ago. Because the frog's primary food is insects, frogs are useful to humans as controllers of insect populations. A frog that appears to be asleep on a stone may suddenly shoot out its tongue and snatch an insect right out of the air. The insect may have been imperceptible to a human, but the frog is able to sense even tiny nearby movements.

The frog's tongue is a formidable weapon. The tongue is attached to the base of the frog's mouth, and the tip of the tongue points backwards toward its throat. When a frog becomes aware of a nearby insect, it can shoot out its tongue instantly and accurately to ensnare the insect. The tongue is coated with sticky mucus that helps catch the prey. The frog swallows its food whole. The frog can use its eyes to help force food down its throat by pulling the eyes far back into the eye sockets. After it eats, the frog may appear to go back to sleep immediately. This is deceptive, however, because if the frog senses another insect flying by, it will wake up and snatch it, too, with its long tongue.

1. **Recognizing Words in Context**

   Find the word *imperceptible* in the passage. One definition below is closest to the meaning of that word. One definition has the opposite or nearly opposite meaning. The remaining definition has a completely different meaning. Label the definitions C for *closest*, O for *opposite or nearly opposite*, and D for *different*.

   _____ a. moving quickly

   _____ b. not noticeable

   _____ c. easy to see

2. **Distinguishing Fact from Opinion**

   Two of the statements below present *facts*, which can be proved correct. The other statement is an *opinion*, which expresses someone's thoughts or beliefs. Label the statements F for *fact* and O for *opinion*.

   _____ a. The frog's sticky tongue helps it catch its prey.

   _____ b. Frogs are one of the animals that are most valuable to humans.

   _____ c. The frog's primary food is insects.

3. Keeping Events in Order

Label the statements below 1, 2, and 3 to show the order in which the events happen.

_____ a. The frog's tongue shoots out of its mouth.

_____ b. The frog senses its prey.

_____ c. The frog swallows its prey.

4. Making Correct Inferences

Two of the statements below are correct *inferences,* or reasonable guesses. They are based on information in the passage. The other statement is an incorrect, or faulty, inference. Label the statements C for *correct* inference and F for *faulty* inference.

_____ a. Frogs eat more insects than other amphibians do.

_____ b. Frogs are able to sense prey nearby, even if their eyes are closed.

_____ c. If frogs were to become extinct, the number of insects would increase.

5. Understanding Main Ideas

One of the statements below expresses the main idea of the passage. One statement is too general, or too broad. The other explains only part of the passage; it is too narrow. Label the statements M for *main idea,* B for *too broad,* and N for *too narrow.*

_____ a. Frogs are a common type of amphibian.

_____ b. The frog's tongue has sticky mucus on it.

_____ c. Frogs have a unique method of capturing prey.

Correct Answers, Part A _____

Correct Answers, Part B _____

Total Correct Answers _____

The Water Cycle

The water cycle is a complex process that constantly recycles Earth's water supply. The water cycle is vital to human survival because only a small percentage of the water on Earth is available for human use. Most water is in the form of salt water in the oceans, and much of the rest of the water is frozen in glaciers and ice caps. The water cycle consists of six basic processes. They are evaporation, condensation, precipitation, infiltration, surface runoff, and transpiration.

Evaporation takes place when a liquid changes into a gas. Temperature is the primary cause of evaporation. The sun's heat changes water into water vapor. When this happens, water vapor ascends into the atmosphere.

Condensation is the process in which a gas is changed into a liquid. Temperature is also a factor here. As temperature drops, water vapor changes to water. When water vapor condenses onto tiny dust particles, clouds are formed. Condensation also produces morning dew.

Certain combinations of temperature and atmospheric pressure cause the small water droplets in clouds to become larger. Eventually they become so large that gravity pulls them to the ground. This is known as precipitation. Precipitation can take the form of rain, snow, sleet, or hail. This is the step in the water cycle in which water is returned to Earth's surface.

Infiltration is the process in which rain and melted snow soaks into the ground through the soil and underlying layers of rock. As water travels through these layers, many of its impurities are filtered out. This groundwater is a major source of drinking water.

Surface runoff occurs when precipitation is not absorbed into the soil. Often this happens because the soil is already saturated with water. The surplus water runs off into streams and rivers. These streams and rivers eventually flow to the ocean. This helps replace the large quantity of water that evaporates from the ocean each day.

Transpiration is the process of evaporation through plant leaves. When plant roots absorb water from the soil, the water travels up through the stems and eventually reaches the leaves. There some of it evaporates during the process of photosynthesis. This adds water vapor to the air. Large forests return a great deal of water to the atmosphere in this manner.

There is no real beginning or end to the water cycle. The six processes occur simultaneously, bringing freshwater to the living things that need it.

Reading Time _____

Recalling Facts

1. The process that recycles Earth's water supply is called
   - ❏ a. precipitation.
   - ❏ b. infiltration.
   - ❏ c. the water cycle.

2. Condensation occurs when
   - ❏ a. a liquid becomes a gas.
   - ❏ b. a gas becomes a liquid.
   - ❏ c. a liquid freezes.

3. The primary factor in evaporation is
   - ❏ a. temperature.
   - ❏ b. altitude.
   - ❏ c. geography.

4. Snow, sleet, and hail are examples of
   - ❏ a. condensation.
   - ❏ b. precipitation.
   - ❏ c. ice cap evaporation.

5. The process of evaporation through plant leaves is called
   - ❏ a. condensation.
   - ❏ b. infiltration.
   - ❏ c. transpiration.

Understanding Ideas

6. One can infer that steam is created by
   - ❏ a. condensation.
   - ❏ b. infiltration.
   - ❏ c. evaporation.

7. One can assume that water will change form quickly if
   - ❏ a. there is no wind.
   - ❏ b. significant temperature change occurs quickly.
   - ❏ c. the air pressure gradually rises.

8. Which of the following provides the best illustration of what happens to water during the infiltration process?
   - ❏ a. gravel being spread along a driveway
   - ❏ b. sand and pebbles pouring into a sieve
   - ❏ c. water flowing from a garden hose

9. One can assume that the reason impurities are filtered out when water flows through underground rock is
   - ❏ a. molecules of impurities are larger than molecules of water.
   - ❏ b. molecules of water are larger than molecules of impurities.
   - ❏ c. underground rock is a factor in transpiration.

10. One can assume from the passage that the water droplets in the clouds are _____ the water droplets that fall to Earth's surface.
    - ❏ a. heavier than
    - ❏ b. lighter than
    - ❏ c. the same weight as

14 | B | Rainmaker: An Experiment

The water cycle is indispensable to life on Earth. If one thinks about the vastness of Earth, it is hard to comprehend the total amount of water continually progressing through the water cycle. The six phases of the water cycle are always occurring simultaneously. The following experiment will demonstrate the concepts underlying three of these phases: evaporation, condensation, and precipitation.

Step One: Gather a large, clear bowl; some plastic wrap; and a small weight. You will also need a small, shallow container, such as a container for potato-chip dip.

Step Two: Place the small container in the center of the bowl.

Step Three: Pour a small amount of water into the bowl, being careful to avoid getting any water in the small container.

Step Four: Cover the bowl with plastic wrap. Wrap the rubber band around the plastic wrap to fasten it to the bowl. Position the weight on top of the plastic wrap, directly above the smaller container.

Step Five: Put the bowl in direct sunlight, either outside in a secure location or on a windowsill.

The water will evaporate and condense into droplets on the underside of the plastic wrap. When the droplets become large enough, they will fall into the small container as rain.

1. **Recognizing Words in Context**

    Find the word *indispensable* in the passage. One definition below is closest to the meaning of that word. One definition has the opposite or nearly opposite meaning. The remaining definition has a completely different meaning. Label the definitions C for *closest,* O for *opposite or nearly opposite,* and D for *different.*

    _____ a. useless

    _____ b. obvious

    _____ c. necessary

2. **Distinguishing Fact from Opinion**

    Two of the statements below present *facts,* which can be proved correct. The other statement is an *opinion,* which expresses someone's thoughts or beliefs. Label the statements F for *fact* and O for *opinion.*

    _____ a. Evaporation is part of the water cycle.

    _____ b. The water cycle is important to Earth.

    _____ c. This rainmaking experiment is an excellent way to understand the water cycle.

3. Keeping Events in Order

Label the statements below 1, 2, and 3 to show the order in which the steps should be performed.

_____ a. Place the bowl in the sun.

_____ b. Check to see how much water has condensed.

_____ c. Put water in the bowl.

4. Making Correct Inferences

Two of the statements below are correct *inferences,* or reasonable guesses. They are based on information in the passage. The other statement is an incorrect, or faulty, inference. Label the statements C for *correct* inference and F for *faulty* inference.

_____ a. Condensation could not occur without evaporation.

_____ b. The rainmaking experiment will make the same amount of rain every time.

_____ c. Direct sunlight speeds the rate of evaporation.

5. Understanding Main Ideas

One of the statements below expresses the main idea of the passage. One statement is too general, or too broad. The other explains only part of the passage; it is too narrow. Label the statements M for *main idea,* B for *too broad,* and N for *too narrow.*

_____ a. The rainmaking experiment requires two containers.

_____ b. The water cycle has several parts.

_____ c. The creation of rain can be demonstrated in an experiment that uses everyday objects.

Correct Answers, Part A _____

Correct Answers, Part B _____

Total Correct Answers _____

68

15 | A | Wetlands

Earth's surface consists of many different types of regions. Among these regions are wetlands. The word *wetlands* does not have a precise definition because wetlands vary so much from place to place. Among the ways in which they differ are in soil, topography, and climate. The main feature of wetlands is saturated soil. This means that the soil is covered by water or water is present at the surface of the soil throughout the year. The presence of water creates a unique type of soil in which dead plants and animal matter decay slowly.

Wetlands are quite common. They are found on every continent except Antarctica. Wetlands can support both water-based and land-based life. Only certain kinds of plants and animals can survive in wetlands. There are two main types of wetlands: inland wetlands and coastal wetlands.

Inland wetlands receive water from precipitation and from groundwater and surface water. An example of an inland wetland is a marsh. Marshes tend to form in areas near the mouths of rivers or where water collects in depressions in the land. The ideal environment for many reeds and grasses, marshes display great biological diversity. Water lilies and cattails are plants commonly found in marshes.

Coastal wetlands are areas that border oceans. They get their freshwater from the same sources that inland wetlands do, but here the freshwater is mixed with ocean water. Coastal wetlands are harsh environments for many plants and animals. The salt water and the movement of the tides continually change the composition of the water so that only salt-tolerant species known as halophytes can survive.

An example of a coastal wetland is a tidal salt marsh. Tidal salt marshes receive water from rivers, runoff, and groundwater, in addition to water from the ocean's tides. The influx of freshwater helps to dilute the salt content of the seawater. The saltwater content of tidal salt marshes affects the number and types of species that can live in this habitat. The salt marsh is home to mussels and oysters. Cordgrass is an example of a plant commonly found in salt marshes. Salt marshes also supply food and a place of refuge for migrating birds, such as ducks and geese.

The expansion of urban and agricultural areas has eliminated many wetlands. Some species of plants and animals that are found only in wetlands have decreased in number.

Reading Time _____

Recalling Facts

1. One continent where wetlands are not found is
   - ❑ a. South America.
   - ❑ b. Antarctica.
   - ❑ c. Africa.

2. An example of a wetland is a
   - ❑ a. mountain lake.
   - ❑ b. reservoir.
   - ❑ c. swamp.

3. The dominant feature of a wetland is
   - ❑ a. ground saturated with water.
   - ❑ b. a mix of salt water and freshwater.
   - ❑ c. a large network of streams.

4. A plant common to a marsh is the
   - ❑ a. huckleberry.
   - ❑ b. cattail.
   - ❑ c. rose.

5. Salt-tolerant species are known as
   - ❑ a. halophytes.
   - ❑ b. angiosperms.
   - ❑ c. electrolytes.

Understanding Ideas

6. One would be most likely to find a wetland near
   - ❑ a. a large body of water.
   - ❑ b. a densely populated area.
   - ❑ c. a coniferous forest.

7. A person that lives near a wetland is most likely to live in a region that
   - ❑ a. has few hills.
   - ❑ b. is near one of the polar regions.
   - ❑ c. is part of the migratory path for birds.

8. One can assume that most wetlands receive water from
   - ❑ a. surface water only.
   - ❑ b. precipitation only.
   - ❑ c. several sources.

9. Compared to inland wetlands, coastal wetlands
   - ❑ a. tend to be found in the Midwestern states.
   - ❑ b. have a higher saltwater content.
   - ❑ c. tend to be easier for plants and animals to adapt to.

10. From the article, you can conclude that what constitutes a wetland
    - ❑ a. mainly involves soil that is saturated with water.
    - ❑ b. is based solely on temperature.
    - ❑ c. is dependent solely on geographic location.

15   B   The Benefits of Wetlands

Wetlands provide many important benefits to our ecosystem. Among these are drinking water purification, fire safety, and protection from storm damage, including floods.

Wetlands help to purify our drinking water. Most of our drinking water comes from groundwater supplies. When water moves through the earth, it passes through many different kinds of plants and soil on its way to the underground reservoirs. Wetlands act as sponges. They naturally filter the water so that when it reaches the groundwater level below, it is cleaner and safer to drink.

Wetlands also help with fire safety. Forest fires can spread very quickly, causing devastating damage over large areas. Wetlands lying within forests do not burn easily. They serve as buffer zones when major fires break out.

Wetlands also help protect communities from severe storms originating over the oceans. Wetlands provide a natural barrier between large storm waves and coastal towns. They also help to decrease the erosion that occurs through the movement of waves and tides. Less erosion of land means more protection from the surging waves of storms.

Wetlands can help control floods. Though flooding is an important ecological process, it can be very damaging to property. Wetlands are able to absorb large amounts of water. This helps to safeguard the cities near flooded areas.

1. **Recognizing Words in Context**

   Find the word *buffer* in the passage. One definition below is closest to the meaning of that word. One definition has the opposite or nearly opposite meaning. The remaining definition has a completely different meaning. Label the definitions C for *closest*, O for *opposite or nearly opposite*, and D for *different*.

   _____ a. protective

   _____ b. exposed

   _____ c. destructive

2. **Distinguishing Fact from Opinion**

   Two of the statements below present *facts*, which can be proved correct. The other statement is an *opinion*, which expresses someone's thoughts or beliefs. Label the statements F for *fact* and O for *opinion*.

   _____ a. Wetlands provide protection from storms.

   _____ b. Wetlands help purify drinking water.

   _____ c. Wetlands are among the most important ecosystems on Earth.

3. Keeping Events in Order

Label the statements below 1, 2, and 3 to show the order in which the events happen.

_____ a. Only a small amount of ocean water flows into a coastal town.

_____ b. As waves crash through a wetland, they lose much of their force.

_____ c. Huge storm waves form at sea.

4. Making Correct Inferences

Two of the statements below are correct *inferences,* or reasonable guesses. They are based on information in the passage. The other statement is an incorrect, or faulty, inference. Label the statements C for *correct* inference and F for *faulty* inference.

_____ a. Property near a wetland cannot be damaged by flooding.

_____ b. Flooding is more severe in coastal towns that have no nearby wetlands.

_____ c. The worst forest fires occur in forests in which there are no wetlands.

5. Understanding Main Ideas

One of the statements below expresses the main idea of the passage. One statement is too general, or too broad. The other explains only part of the passage; it is too narrow. Label the statements M for *main idea,* B for *too broad,* and N for *too narrow.*

_____ a. Wetlands provide several benefits to the areas around them.

_____ b. Wetlands help prevent the spread of forest fires.

_____ c. Wetlands are unique ecosystems.

Correct Answers, Part A _____

Correct Answers, Part B _____

Total Correct Answers _____

16   A   Glaciers

A glacier is a mass formed of ice, air, water, and sediments. A glacier can be large enough to cover a continent or small enough to fill a valley between two hills. Glaciers are not found only in the Arctic and Antarctic. New Zealand, Chile, and the northern United States, among other places, have glaciers. Most glaciers exist at high altitudes where temperatures are cooler. In order for a glacier to endure, the temperature must be cold enough that more ice accumulates than melts. Therefore, temperature and precipitation are two key factors for glacier formation.

Glaciers form due to evaporation and condensation within dense snowpacks. Over time, the snow changes to glacial ice. The melting and refreezing of ice and snow contributes to this process. Because glaciers form over a long period of time, they can provide valuable information to scientists about past climate variations. For example, scientists have concluded that the ice below the surface at the South Pole is 1,000 years old. The ice contains air bubbles from Earth's atmosphere 1,000 years ago. An analysis of this air can reveal information about Earth's history.

Glaciers move, though very slowly. Movement ranges from a few meters to thousands of meters per year. The movement of glaciers has helped form the terrain of many areas. When glaciers move, they sculpt the land, moving material from one location to another. Many of our current mountain ranges were formed over millions of years by glacial flow. Other mountain ranges were flattened by glaciers.

A glacial system has two zones, the accumulation zone and the ablation zone. As a rule, the accumulation zone is found at the top of a glacier. Accumulation is the addition of material, such as snow and rain, to the mass of the glacier. Hence, the accumulation zone is the area of a glacier where new material is being added to the mass faster than ice is being lost.

The ablation zone is usually found at the edges of the glacier. Ablation is the loss of ice mass from a glacier. Ablation can take place through melting at the surface or the base, through evaporation, or through calving, which is the breaking off of icebergs. The ablation zone is where more mass is being lost than gained. If a glacier is growing, the accumulation zone is greater than the ablation zone; if a glacier is shrinking, then ablation is greater than accumulation.

Reading Time _____

Recalling Facts

1. _____ are the source of the ice in glaciers.
   - ❏ a. Icebergs
   - ❏ b. Arctic lakes
   - ❏ c. Snowpacks

2. Calving happens when
   - ❏ a. icebergs break off from glaciers.
   - ❏ b. icebergs grow to become glaciers.
   - ❏ c. a glacier attaches to another glacier.

3. The process in which material is removed from a glacier is called
   - ❏ a. interference.
   - ❏ b. ablation.
   - ❏ c. accumulation.

4. Two key factors for the endurance of a glacier are precipitation and
   - ❏ a. time of year.
   - ❏ b. temperature.
   - ❏ c. size of a body of water.

5. The accumulation zone is found _____ of a glacier.
   - ❏ a. at the top
   - ❏ b. at the bottom
   - ❏ c. in the middle

Understanding Ideas

6. Glaciers in areas that have warm summers are likely to be _____ glaciers in Antarctica.
   - ❏ a. larger than
   - ❏ b. smaller than
   - ❏ c. about the same size as

7. One would be most likely to see a glacier
   - ❏ a. in a valley in Minnesota.
   - ❏ b. in a mountain range in Canada.
   - ❏ c. alongside a forest in California.

8. The melting of a glacier during a period of unusually warm weather would be an example of
   - ❏ a. ablation.
   - ❏ b. accumulation.
   - ❏ c. calving.

9. The oldest material in a glacier would most likely be found
   - ❏ a. near the top of the glacier.
   - ❏ b. toward the middle of the west end of the glacier.
   - ❏ c. near the bottom of the center of the glacier.

10. Along with air bubbles, what would glaciers be most likely to contain that would provide valuable information to scientists?
    - ❏ a. well-preserved bodies of dead animals
    - ❏ b. large meteorites from Mars and other planets
    - ❏ c. layers that contain liquid water and rare fish

The Ice Age

Over the course of Earth's history, there have been several ice ages. The most recent one began about 3 million years ago. A number of factors can lead to the start of an ice age. Two key causes involve plate tectonics and changes in Earth's orbit. Plate tectonics may be the more important cause. Plate movements can push up large areas of continents. This can bring about extreme changes in global oceanic and atmospheric circulation patterns. When circulation patterns change, the climate can change, often drastically. Tectonic shifts typically take place over millions of years. For instance, about 3.5 million years ago, the Isthmus of Panama was formed. This isthmus stopped the east-west ocean circulation in the area. This, in turn, caused the Gulf Stream to grow stronger, which produced warmer water in the Northern Hemisphere. The warmer weather increased precipitation over the North Pole, causing ice sheets to form and expand.

Changes in Earth's orbit over time also help to cause ice ages. These changes affect the way solar radiation is dispersed over Earth's surface. When the orbit becomes more elliptical, the difference in winter and summer temperatures in the Northern Hemisphere increases. Extremes in the seasons of the Southern Hemisphere decrease. Glaciers can begin forming in northern areas, heralding the dawn of a new ice age.

1. **Recognizing Words in Context**

    Find the word *dispersed* in the passage. One definition below is closest to the meaning of that word. One definition has the opposite or nearly opposite meaning. The remaining definition has a completely different meaning. Label the definitions C for *closest*, O for *opposite or nearly opposite*, and D for *different*.

    _____ a. deflected

    _____ b. distributed

    _____ c. collected

2. **Distinguishing Fact from Opinion**

    Two of the statements below present *facts*, which can be proved correct. The other statement is an *opinion*, which expresses someone's thoughts or beliefs. Label the statements F for *fact* and O for *opinion*.

    _____ a. Tectonic changes generally occur over millions of years.

    _____ b. Human beings would have no problem adapting to a new ice age.

    _____ c. When precipitation increases over the North Pole, ice sheets begin to form and spread.

3. Keeping Events in Order

Label the statements below 1, 2, and 3 to show the order in which the events happen.

_____ a. Plate movements cause an uplift of continental blocks.

_____ b. The climate changes dramatically.

_____ c. Atmospheric circulation patterns begin to change.

4. Making Correct Inferences

Two of the statements below are correct *inferences,* or reasonable guesses. They are based on information in the passage. The other statement is an incorrect, or faulty, inference. Label the statements C for *correct* inference and F for *faulty* inference.

_____ a. An ice age is likely to occur again.

_____ b. Future ice ages won't be as extreme as past ones.

_____ c. There have been many small changes in Earth's orbit.

5. Understanding Main Ideas

One of the statements below expresses the main idea of the passage. One statement is too general, or too broad. The other explains only part of the passage; it is too narrow. Label the statements M for *main idea,* B for *too broad,* and N for *too narrow.*

_____ a. The most recent ice age began about 3 million years ago.

_____ b. Drastic changes sometimes occur in Earth's climate.

_____ c. Plate tectonics and changes in Earth's orbit are two important factors in the occurrence of an ice age.

Correct Answers, Part A _____

Correct Answers, Part B _____

Total Correct Answers _____

Careers in Zoology

Zoology is a branch of biology that encompasses many smaller areas of study. Zoologists are biologists who specialize in the study of animal life. Some of the animal topics that zoologists study include life processes, behavior, evolution, growth, habitats, conservation, and classification. One zoologist might study the eating habits of cougars. Another might focus on wildlife preservation in Alaska. Still others might work in museums or laboratories doing research.

Of course, a zoologist could also work in a zoo. Working in a zoo provides a zoologist with the opportunity to work closely with animals. It also gives the zoologist the chance to study individual animals over a long period of time. This serves as a valuable source of research data to the zoologist, who can learn how to create exhibits that are better for both animals and visitors. Animals also benefit from having the same zookeeper for an extended period, as the zoologist learns their particular needs and behaviors and is able to quickly recognize when they are sick.

Anthrozoology is the study of interactions between animals and humans. Anthrozoologists draw on knowledge from such fields as zoology, psychology, medicine, veterinary science, and social science. Anthrozoology is a fairly new field of study that has developed in part because people's attitudes toward animals have changed in the past few decades. Some of the issues that anthrozoologists study are the animal rights movement, the evolution of zoos, the raising of farm animals, and the use of animals in medical research.

Humans and animals often depend on each other. This is evident in people's relationships with their pets. Cats and dogs provide company for many people. One of the things an anthrozoologist may do is compare and contrast message signals; for example, cat-to-cat messages versus cat-to-human messages. Other types of research might involve observing guide dogs and how they help their owners physically and emotionally or looking at the differences between the ways free-range horses and pastured horses play. Anthrozoology is such a new field of study that not many universities offer academic programs devoted specifically to it. Some people study anthrozoology as part of a graduate program in zoology or a related field.

Zookeepers and anthrozoologists are just two of the many kinds of zoologists. Careers in zoology will take on greater importance as more animals become threatened species and as scientific research about animals sheds more light on humans and human society.

Reading Time _____

Recalling Facts

1. Zoology is the study of
   - ❏ a. zoos.
   - ❏ b. animals.
   - ❏ c. people.

2. The study of the interaction between animals and humans is called
   - ❏ a. anthrozoology.
   - ❏ b. biozoology.
   - ❏ c. anthrobiology.

3. Zoology is a branch of
   - ❏ a. biology.
   - ❏ b. botany.
   - ❏ c. psychology.

4. Some zoologists focus on
   - ❏ a. weather patterns.
   - ❏ b. animal conservation.
   - ❏ c. wind erosion.

5. Anthrozoologists are especially interested in
   - ❏ a. animal anatomy.
   - ❏ b. wild dogs.
   - ❏ c. pets.

Understanding Ideas

6. One can conclude from the article that careers in zoology
   - ❏ a. are quite similar.
   - ❏ b. encompass a variety of skills and areas of study.
   - ❏ c. are learned "on the job" with little formal education.

7. Compared with other zoologists, an anthrozoologist
   - ❏ a. would be less likely to observe animals in a person's home.
   - ❏ b. is generally more interested in the ways people and animals influence each other.
   - ❏ c. is less likely to study sociology or psychology.

8. One of the most important characteristics a zoologist could have would be
   - ❏ a. a dedication to and concern for animals.
   - ❏ b. several college degrees.
   - ❏ c. teaching experience.

9. An additional benefit of having the same zookeeper working with animals over an extended period of time would be that the animals
   - ❏ a. would behave like pets.
   - ❏ b. would get used to their keeper and be less anxious.
   - ❏ c. would live much longer.

10. It is most likely that an anthrozoologist would conduct a study about
    - ❏ a. mold growth in buildings built prior to 1940.
    - ❏ b. the physical features of gorillas in their natural environment.
    - ❏ c. the uses of rescue dogs.

Zookeepers are the people directly responsible for the care of zoo animals. Large zoos have an entire staff of zookeepers, each responsible for a particular group of animals or section of the zoo. The job responsibilities of a zookeeper can be divided into three main duties: feeding, sanitation, and observation. All are important to the animals' health and well-being.

Feeding the animals correctly requires precision and organization. Every animal has its own particular diet. Some zoos have large kitchen facilities in which specially trained chefs prepare the food by following guidelines developed by the zoo veterinarian. Keepers must make sure each animal gets the right type and amount of food.

Cleaning up after the animals may not sound like fun. But it is vital to the health of the animals. All the habitats and cages must be kept clean. If they aren't, the animals will be more likely to contract illnesses.

Observation of the animals is a job that may not sound important. But over time, the zookeepers get to know the animals well. Because they watch the animals every day, they may very well be the first to notice if one is sick. The keepers can tell the zoo vet what they have observed. This information may help the animal recover more quickly or even save its life.

1. **Recognizing Words in Context**

   Find the word *sanitation* in the passage. One definition below is closest to the meaning of that word. One definition has the opposite or nearly opposite meaning. The remaining definition has a completely different meaning. Label the definitions C for *closest*, O for *opposite or nearly opposite*, and D for *different*.

   _____ a. helping

   _____ b. cleaning

   _____ c. polluting

2. **Distinguishing Fact from Opinion**

   Two of the statements below present *facts*, which can be proved correct. The other statement is an *opinion*, which expresses someone's thoughts or beliefs. Label the statements F for *fact* and O for *opinion*.

   _____ a. The best zookeepers are always kind and gentle with the animals.

   _____ b. Zoo animals are fed special diets.

   _____ c. Careless zoo keeping can endanger the health of the animals.

3. Keeping Events in Order

Label the statements below 1, 2, and 3 to show the order in which the events happen.

_____ a. The zookeeper notifies the zoo veterinarian.

_____ b. The zookeeper notices that a usually active lion stops moving around its habitat.

_____ c. The veterinarian determines that the lion has an infection.

4. Making Correct Inferences

Two of the statements below are correct *inferences,* or reasonable guesses. They are based on information in the passage. The other statement is an incorrect, or faulty, inference. Label the statements C for *correct* inference and F for *faulty* inference.

_____ a. Zookeepers must know as much about medicine as vets do.

_____ b. Animals depend mainly on their zookeeper for their well-being.

_____ c. Zookeepers know the animals they work with better than anyone else does.

5. Understanding Main Ideas

One of the statements below expresses the main idea of the passage. One statement is too general, or too broad. The other explains only part of the passage; it is too narrow. Label the statements M for *main idea*, B for *too broad*, and N for *too narrow.*

_____ a. Many different people work at a zoo.

_____ b. The zookeeper has many responsibilities in caring for the animals.

_____ c. A sick animal may need care from the zoo veterinarian.

Correct Answers, Part A _____

Correct Answers, Part B _____

Total Correct Answers _____

80

Perhaps your nose is the same shape as your mother's. Maybe you have your father's eyes. Or you might not look much like either of your parents but very much like one of your grandparents. These similarities and differences can be attributed to heredity. Heredity is the passing on of biological traits from one generation to another. Nose shape and eye color are just two traits among hundreds.

The study of heredity is called genetics. Gregor Mendel, an Austrian monk, conducted extensive experiments in the mid-1800s that created a mathematical foundation for the development of genetics. Mendel was interested in patterns of inheritance. His experiments involved pea plants. Prior to Mendel's work, people thought that all of the hereditary information in parents was blended together in their children. Mendel showed each plant transmits only about half of its genetic information to its offspring. Further, he showed that the information is transmitted in separate units and that each offspring receives a somewhat different set of units. His work was published in 1866, but at first it was largely ignored by the scientific community. It was not until 1900 that Mendel's work became well known; in that year several scientists published papers that showed the importance of his research.

Over the next few decades, scientists located the microscopic structures responsible for the results described by Mendel. They found that cells contain thin strands called chromosomes. Chromosomes are made of protein and deoxyribonucleic acid, or DNA. The chemical parts of DNA can be arranged in different ways. A gene is a particular pattern of DNA chemicals associated with a specific biological trait. There are 23 pairs of chromosomes in a human cell. Each chromosome has several hundred to several thousand genes.

In most cases, there are two genes for every trait. One gene comes from the mother. The other gene comes from the father. Some genes are dominant and some are recessive. When parents contribute genes with different characteristics for the same trait—for example, blue eyes and brown eyes—whichever gene is dominant is the one whose characteristic will be visible in the child.

Though genes are responsible for physical characteristics, they do not account for all of a person's characteristics. The environment also is important in determining what a person is like. For example, a child may inherit athletic ability. But that ability may not become apparent unless the child receives both proper nutrition and encouragement.

Reading Time _____

Recalling Facts

1. The passing on of biological traits from one generation to another is called
   - ❑ a. chromosomes.
   - ❑ b. environmental determinism.
   - ❑ c. heredity.

2. Gregor Mendel first performed trait-inheritance experiments using
   - ❑ a. pea plants.
   - ❑ b. fruit flies.
   - ❑ c. bread mold.

3. Mendel showed that each plant passes on _____ of its genetic information to its offspring.
   - ❑ a. 25 percent
   - ❑ b. 50 percent
   - ❑ c. 90 percent

4. Genes consist of patterns of
   - ❑ a. recessive characteristics.
   - ❑ b. chromosomes.
   - ❑ c. DNA chemical parts.

5. Human cells have _____ pairs of chromosomes.
   - ❑ a. 13
   - ❑ b. 33
   - ❑ c. 23

Understanding Ideas

6. If you have freckles but your parents do not, the most likely conclusion is
   - ❑ a. your parents do not carry the gene for freckles.
   - ❑ b. there is no gene for freckles.
   - ❑ c. your parents each carry recessive genes for freckles.

7. The article suggests that heredity
   - ❑ a. is entirely responsible for physical characteristics.
   - ❑ b is partly responsible for physical characteristics.
   - ❑ c. is responsible for about half of a person's physical characteristics.

8. If one parent passes on a gene for brown eye color and the other parent passes on a gene for green eye color, and a child's eyes are green, you can assume that
   - ❑ a. the gene for green eyes is recessive.
   - ❑ b. the gene for brown eyes is dominant.
   - ❑ c. the gene for green eyes is dominant.

9. Scientists would be most likely to use DNA research to
   - ❑ a. determine if a baby carried a gene for multiple sclerosis.
   - ❑ b. analyze herbal medicines.
   - ❑ c. help parents determine how to discipline their children.

10. The number of people _____ would probably be least affected by advances in genetic research.
    - ❑ a. with Alzheimer's disease
    - ❑ b. who serve in the military
    - ❑ c. with poor vision

There are two types of twins: identical and fraternal. Identical twins, also called monozygotic twins, are formed from a single egg. They are always of the same gender, and they share an identical genetic makeup. Fraternal, or dizygotic twins, are formed from two separate eggs. These twins share only 25 percent of their genes, just like any brother and sister. One half of fraternal twins are boy-girl, one quarter are girl-girl, and one quarter are boy-boy.

Identical twins generally tend to be emotionally closer to one another than fraternal twins. They also tend to develop psychologically in similar ways. Many identical twins claim to be able to tell when their sibling is in pain or danger, even if the sibling is far away. Fraternal twins, however, find it easier to establish unique identities and develop on their own. This may be due to their being more clearly different, physically and emotionally, from each other. Identical twins who differ in size at birth may have birth defects. Also, if one identical twin develops a disease, it is likely that the other twin has a tendency toward the same disease. Many of these statements are generalizations, however. It is possible for fraternal twins to be very close and for identical twins to have antipathy toward each other. The potential for variation in human characteristics is almost infinite.

1. **Recognizing Words in Context**

   Find the word *antipathy* in the passage. One definition below is closest to the meaning of that word. One definition has the opposite or nearly opposite meaning. The remaining definition has a completely different meaning. Label the definitions C for *closest*, O for *opposite or nearly opposite*, and D for *different*.

   _____ a. love

   _____ b. separation

   _____ c. dislike

2. **Distinguishing Fact from Opinion**

   Two of the statements below present *facts*, which can be proved correct. The other statement is an *opinion*, which expresses someone's thoughts or beliefs. Label the statements F for *fact* and O for *opinion*.

   _____ a. Identical twins are always the same gender.

   _____ b. The similarities in identical twins is fascinating.

   _____ c. Fraternal twins share 25 percent of their genes.

3. Keeping Events in Order

Label the statements below 1, 2, and 3 to show the order in which the events happen.

_____ a. A doctor determines that two embryos are developing from a single egg.

_____ b. Twins develop freckles at the same time.

_____ c. Twins are born.

4. Making Correct Inferences

Two of the statements below are correct *inferences*, or reasonable guesses. They are based on information in the passage. The other statement is an incorrect, or faulty, inference. Label the statements C for *correct* inference and F for *faulty* inference.

_____ a. If one fraternal twin has leukemia, the other twin will eventually develop it too.

_____ b. Identical twins often share the same likes and dislikes.

_____ c. Fraternal twins are most likely to be boy-girl pairs.

5. Understanding Main Ideas

One of the statements below expresses the main idea of the passage. One statement is too general, or too broad. The other explains only part of the passage; it is too narrow. Label the statements M for *main idea*, B for *too broad*, and N for *too narrow*.

_____ a. Twins formed from two separate eggs are called dizygotic.

_____ b. Identical twins differ from fraternal twins in a number of ways.

_____ c. Sometimes mothers give birth to more than one baby at a time.

Correct Answers, Part A _____

Correct Answers, Part B _____

Total Correct Answers _____

Computers and the Information Revolution

The Internet has changed people's lives. Advances in computer technology have made a seemingly endless supply of information and ideas readily available. Computers have also provided new forms of communication to help circulate this information. Electronic mail, commonly known as e-mail, allows millions of people to communicate easily and efficiently.

The scientific world also has benefited greatly from the speed and ease of electronic transmissions. One example involved the January 26, 2001, earthquake in western India. This earthquake, which measured 7.6 on the Richter scale, killed about 20,000 people and destroyed about 350,000 homes. Damage was particularly heavy in the city of Bhuj, and the quake came to be known as the Bhuj earthquake. The Bhuj quake, unlike most earthquakes of its magnitude, did not rupture Earth's surface. It was a rare intraplate quake, which means it did not originate along the edges of the plates that form Earth's crust. The epicenter of the quake was in an uninhabited, desolate area. Collecting data about the quake would have been very difficult without the use of computerized equipment. The Internet allowed scientists to quickly transmit data about the quake to universities and research centers around the world. Earthquake experts could provide important insight into the quake's origin and effects without having to travel to the faraway site and personally gather the information they needed.

The Internet has also helped in research activities that are not as urgent as earthquake analysis. People have created databases of research findings in the social sciences and many other fields. These databases are contained on Web sites that are quickly and easily accessible. The Internet also helps scientists working far apart to form a connected community. Scholars can use e-mail to engage in dialogue with other people working in their fields without the expense of travel or long-distance phone calls. This can make their research efforts more efficient and focused. Electronic mailing lists can help people to locate others with whom they can share information and opinions about common interests. This can help people work together to come up with ideas they might never have had individually.

Along with advances in computer technology have come abuses of its capabilities. Anyone skilled in computer programming and computer languages is capable of doing a great deal of harm through the Internet and e-mail. Hoaxes, viruses, and electronic theft are just some of the problems that have emerged.

Reading Time _____

Recalling Facts

1. The term *e-mail* is short for
   - ❏ a. extremely fast mail.
   - ❏ b. electronic mail.
   - ❏ c. efficient mail.

2. Large databases can be stored on
   - ❏ a. Web sites.
   - ❏ b. search engines.
   - ❏ c. monitors.

3. One way that e-mail helps build community among scholars is by
   - ❏ a. performing complex mathematical analysis.
   - ❏ b. providing low-cost communication.
   - ❏ c. serving as the main way of publishing experimental data.

4. In January 2001 a major earthquake hit
   - ❏ a. western India.
   - ❏ b. northern Afghanistan.
   - ❏ c. eastern Iran.

5. Computer technology was helpful in analyzing the Bhuj earthquake because
   - ❏ a. scientists used computer programs to accurately predict the date of the quake.
   - ❏ b. city planners used computers to design earthquake-proof buildings.
   - ❏ c. the epicenter of the quake was in a remote area.

Understanding Ideas

6. From the article, one can infer that prior to the widespread availability of the Internet, scholars
   - ❏ a. more often duplicated the projects of other scholars.
   - ❏ b. did not communicate with scholars on other continents.
   - ❏ c. had to send e-mail by satellite.

7. The Internet was probably most useful to seismologists studying the Bhuj quake because they could
   - ❏ a. access the information using various search engines.
   - ❏ b. exchange information with great speed from far away.
   - ❏ c. learn new research methods.

8. The use of computers and the Internet will probably _____ the communication practices among scientists in the future.
   - ❏ a. hinder
   - ❏ b. expand
   - ❏ c. not affect

9. Internet databases would be most useful to
   - ❏ a. a person creating a new computer language.
   - ❏ b. a high school student sending an e-mail to a cousin.
   - ❏ c. a psychology professor doing a survey of brain research.

10. You can infer that an important current activity on the Internet is
    - ❏ a. creating secure databases for financial information.
    - ❏ b. the invention of the World Wide Web.
    - ❏ c. making e-mail available to large U.S. cities.

Voice Synthesizers

Computers and technology are helping people with disabilities to lead more productive and fulfilling lives. One of the computer devices that has benefited them the most is the voice synthesizer. This device can both read text aloud and understand speech.

Some voice synthesizer systems can be programmed to recognize a specific voice. This allows people with paralyzed arms to use computers. It can also help people who have carpal tunnel syndrome, a painful muscle condition that makes it difficult to use a mouse or keyboard.

People who are blind or have impaired vision can use voice synthesizers to read what is on a computer screen. Advanced voice synthesizers can also act as substitute voices for people who have trouble communicating verbally.

A scanner that has optical character recognition can read and store printed material electronically. It can be connected to a voice synthesizer that reads aloud the text that is stored in the scanner. Voice synthesizers can be helpful for people who spend a great deal of time at the computer. Writers and journalists can benefit from this tool. Office workers can also use it. Sitting in front of a computer and inputting with a keyboard all day is hard on the back, neck, and wrists. Voice synthesizers may eventually replace keyboards on some computers.

1. **Recognizing Words in Context**

   Find the word *impaired* in the passage. One definition below is closest to the meaning of that word. One definition has the opposite or nearly opposite meaning. The remaining definition has a completely different meaning. Label the definitions C for *closest*, O for *opposite or nearly opposite*, and D for *different*.

   _____ a. defective

   _____ b. multiple

   _____ c. flawless

2. **Distinguishing Fact from Opinion**

   Two of the statements below present *facts*, which can be proved correct. The other statement is an *opinion*, which expresses someone's thoughts or beliefs. Label the statements F for *fact* and O for *opinion*.

   _____ a. Voice synthesizers can read computer text to people.

   _____ b. Voice synthesizers can produce substitute voices.

   _____ c. Voice synthesizers are one of the best uses of technology.

3. Keeping Events in Order

Label the statements below 1, 2, and 3 to show the order in which the events happen.

_____ a. A student is once again able to participate fully in class.

_____ b. A student obtains a voice synthesizer.

_____ c. A student loses her speaking ability as the result of a car accident.

4. Making Correct Inferences

Two of the statements below are correct *inferences,* or reasonable guesses. They are based on information in the passage. The other statement is an incorrect, or faulty, inference. Label the statements C for *correct* inference and F for *faulty* inference.

_____ a. Voice synthesizers will eventually make human speech unnecessary.

_____ b. If a person's back and neck are aching from using a computer, a voice synthesizer may be helpful.

_____ c. Voice synthesizers are likely to become more widely used in the future.

5. Understanding Main Ideas

One of the statements below expresses the main idea of the passage. One statement is too general, or too broad. The other explains only part of the passage; it is too narrow. Label the statements M for *main idea,* B for *too broad,* and N for *too narrow.*

_____ a. Voice synthesizers can read aloud the information that is on a computer screen.

_____ b. Voice synthesizers can help people in several ways.

_____ c. A variety of electronic devices are designed for people with disabilities.

Correct Answers, Part A _____

Correct Answers, Part B _____

Total Correct Answers _____

Animals have many ways of adapting to their environment to improve their chances for survival. One of the most effective methods is the use of camouflage. Camouflage is defined as the coloring, body shape, or behavior that animals use to conceal themselves. Camouflage can work in two ways: camouflaged prey can hide from predators, and camouflaged predators can sneak up on prey.

There are many examples of camouflage in the animal kingdom. A creature may have a solid body color that matches its environment. Grasshoppers may be green, brown, or gray, depending on their habitat. A polar bear blends into its snowy environment so that seals, its favorite meal, have trouble seeing it when they come up to the surface of the water. Likewise, a sand-colored Fennec fox blends into its desert environment.

An animal's skin or fur may have a pattern that functions as camouflage. A fawn has spots on its fur. When its mother is away, the fawn may lie down on the forest floor. Its spots resemble patches of sunlight created when the sun's rays come streaming through the trees.

A lesser-known type of camouflage is called countershading. This means the animal's body is dark on top and light on the bottom. Since daylight comes from above, the underside of an animal appears to be darker. Countershading lessens this effect, making the outline of an animal's body less recognizable. This coloration also works in a different way for animals in the water. Predators looking down on a swimming animal will see only the dark top of its body which will blend in with the depths of the water. Predators below will look up and see the animal's lighter underside, which blends in with sunlight. Examples of animals that use countershading are white-tailed deer, Canada geese, and largemouth bass.

A "copycat" is an animal with a body structure that imitates some aspect of its environment. The insect known as the walking stick looks like a twig. It can sit on a branch escaping attention until it begins to move. When a butterfly closes its wings, it looks like a leaf. In the rain forest, a sloth turns green during the wettest season. This helps it blend in with the trees in which it lives. The green color actually comes from algae growing on the sloth's fur. Usually animals that blend into their surroundings keep still during the daylight to avoid detection.

Reading Time _____

Recalling Facts

1. The primary purpose of camouflage is to
   - ❑ a. allow an animal to sleep without being disturbed.
   - ❑ b. improve an animal's chances of survival.
   - ❑ c. allow a predator to imitate its prey.

2. An animal that has a patterned coat that serves as camouflage is the
   - ❑ a. Canada goose.
   - ❑ b. sloth.
   - ❑ c. fawn.

3. Camouflage in which an animal's body is dark on top and light on the bottom is called
   - ❑ a. countershading.
   - ❑ b. stripes.
   - ❑ c. patterning.

4. An example of an animal that uses copycat camouflage is a
   - ❑ a. polar bear.
   - ❑ b. walking stick.
   - ❑ c. white-tailed deer.

5. The color of a grasshopper depends on the color of its
   - ❑ a. predators.
   - ❑ b. larvae.
   - ❑ c. habitat.

Understanding Ideas

6. A person who is standing in a stream and fishing is most likely to see animals that have
   - ❑ a. bright colors.
   - ❑ b. countershading.
   - ❑ c. copycat camouflage.

7. The article suggests that camouflage is
   - ❑ a. useful for both predator and prey.
   - ❑ b. mostly useful for prey.
   - ❑ c. mostly useful for predators.

8. From the information in the article, one might conclude that a sloth is
   - ❑ a. active both during the day and at night.
   - ❑ b. less active at night.
   - ❑ c. more active at night.

9. If a butterfly wanted to avoid being seen, it would most likely
   - ❑ a. fly away.
   - ❑ b. fold up its wings.
   - ❑ c. spread its wings

10. What would be a likely reason that a seal cannot stay underwater all the time to avoid polar bears?
    - ❑ a. The seal has lungs and must breathe above the surface of the water.
    - ❑ b. The seal obtains some of its food on land.
    - ❑ c. Sea water can get extremely cold, and the seal needs to come to the surface to warm up.

The Misunderstood Chameleon

Scientific research has uncovered some common misconceptions about animals. Such misconceptions are hard to extirpate because they have been passed down from generation to generation and repeated in numerous sources. One such misconception involves the reason chameleons change color.

The chameleon is a solitary reptile found mainly in southern Africa. It is a tree-dwelling lizard with several notable traits. One trait is its ability to change color. Most chameleons are colored in a way that blends in well with their surroundings. This led people to assume that when a chameleon changes color, it is because it has moved to a different location and needs to blend in with a new background. Scientists have shown this to be a myth. The factors involved in a chameleon's color change are temperature, light, and emotion. For example, when a male chameleon sees another male invading its territory, it may slowly turn black with rage. Most chameleons have a base color of green, brown, or yellow.

Another of the chameleon's traits is its tongue, which it uses to catch insects in a way similar to the way frogs do. When the chameleon spots its prey, it flicks its tongue out to catch it. One side of the chameleon's tongue is sticky for that purpose. Fully extended, the chameleon's tongue is as long as its body.

1. **Recognizing Words in Context**

   Find the word *extirpate* in the passage. One definition below is closest to the meaning of that word. One definition has the opposite or nearly opposite meaning. The remaining definition has a completely different meaning. Label the definitions C for *closest*, O for *opposite or nearly opposite*, and D for *different*.

   _____ a. exceed

   _____ b. support

   _____ c. eliminate

2. **Distinguishing Fact from Opinion**

   Two of the statements below present *facts*, which can be proved correct. The other statement is an *opinion*, which expresses someone's thoughts or beliefs. Label the statements F for *fact* and O for *opinion*.

   _____ a. Chameleons are reptiles.

   _____ b. Chameleons are hideous.

   _____ c. Chameleons have been misunderstood.

3. Keeping Events in Order

Label the statements below 1, 2, and 3 to show the order in which the events happen.

_____ a. A chameleon is sitting near the top of a tall tree on a cloudy day.

_____ b. The chameleon changes color.

_____ c. The sun comes out and the temperature goes up.

4. Making Correct Inferences

Two of the statements below are correct *inferences*, or reasonable guesses. They are based on information in the passage. The other statement is an incorrect, or faulty, inference. Label the statements C for *correct* inference and F for *faulty* inference.

_____ a. Chameleons are not usually black in color.

_____ b. The chameleon is able to flick its tongue quickly and accurately.

_____ c. Chameleons change color in one or two seconds.

5. Understanding Main Ideas

One of the statements below expresses the main idea of the passage. One statement is too general, or too broad. The other explains only part of the passage; it is too narrow. Label the statements M for *main idea*, B for *too broad*, and N for *too narrow*.

_____ a. Chameleons are tree-dwelling lizards.

_____ b. Chameleon possess a number of unusual traits.

_____ c. Some chameleons are yellow.

Correct Answers, Part A _____

Correct Answers, Part B _____

Total Correct Answers _____

The life cycle of a flowering plant begins, simply enough, with a seed. Scientists refer to flowering plants as angiosperms, and they refer to the sprouting of a seed as germination. If a seed germinates too early, too late, or in the wrong environment, the plant embryo will die. A plant embryo is entirely dependent on stored energy until it pushes up through the soil into the sunlight. The stored energy is activated by environmental factors such as the ratio of light to dark, temperature, and the amount of available moisture. All of these properties work to help the seed sprout at a time when it has the greatest opportunity for survival. Once the plant embryo penetrates the surface of the soil, photosynthesis begins to provide it with energy. Photosynthesis is the process through which leaves absorb light energy from the sun to generate food for the plant.

The next step in an angiosperm's life cycle is the development of the seedling. When the embryo emerges above the ground, it continues to grow toward the sun. Soon leaves begin to spread out. As the main stem is pushing up toward the sun, the seedling is pushing roots down into the soil. Roots help stabilize the plant and keep it connected to the ground. They also provide water and minerals to the rest of the plant.

The bud is the beginning of the flowering sequence of an angiosperm. Flower bud development occurs while the plant is still in an immature stage of growth. When the flower appears, the plant has reached maturity and entered the reproductive phase of its life cycle.

A flower contains both a male part, which produces pollen, and a female part, which receives pollen. Bees and other insects are often seen hovering around flowering plants in the spring and summer. This is because the plants have an interdependent relationship with insects. The plant uses the flower's fragrance or color to attract insects. The insects transfer pollen from one plant to another. Pollination also occurs through the action of wind, which can carry the pollen over great distances. Once pollination takes place, the flower begins to make new seeds. This is called fertilization. The next step is seed dispersal. As the flower begins to die, new seeds appear, which must be distributed so that the species can continue. When a seed finds a favorable location, germination begins anew.

Reading Time _____

Recalling Facts

1. _____ is the scientific name for a flowering plant.
   - ❑ a. Gymnosperm
   - ❑ b. Angiosperm
   - ❑ c. Sporophyte

2. A germinating seed is completely dependent upon
   - ❑ a. stored energy.
   - ❑ b. rainfall.
   - ❑ c. fertilizer.

3. Plants get water and minerals from
   - ❑ a. buds.
   - ❑ b. leaves.
   - ❑ c. roots.

4. The reproductive phase of a flowering plant's life cycle begins with the appearance of a
   - ❑ a. flower.
   - ❑ b. seedling.
   - ❑ c. bud.

5. Pollen is transported by
   - ❑ a. water and insects.
   - ❑ b. insects and wind.
   - ❑ c. water and wind.

Understanding Ideas

6. Which of the following statements is most likely true?
   - ❑ a. Insects randomly select which types of flowers they pollinate.
   - ❑ b. Pollination can cause damage to flowers.
   - ❑ c. A strong perfume often attracts insects.

7. The article suggests that flowering plants
   - ❑ a. have predictable life cycles.
   - ❑ b. are equally fragile during every stage of growth.
   - ❑ c. derive their most essential nutrients from animals.

8. The article suggests that
   - ❑ a. all seeds become flowers.
   - ❑ b. only angiosperms grow seeds.
   - ❑ c. several conditions are required for germination to be successful.

9. Which of the following would be most likely to prevent a seed from germinating?
   - ❑ a. high temperatures
   - ❑ b. dry conditions
   - ❑ c. a lack of insects

10. A lack of sunlight would most strongly affect an adult plant's
    - ❑ a. water supply.
    - ❑ b. food supply.
    - ❑ c. mineral supply.

21 B The Sea Anemone

The sea anemone is an unusual sea creature. It looks like a plant, but it is
really a type of meat-eating animal called a polyp. The sea anemone attaches
one end of its cylindrical body to rocks or wood. Anemones can be found
in every ocean and at all depths. Many are colored in brilliant shades of
blue, green, pink, or red. Their coloring is one of the reasons they are often
mistaken for plants.

The sea anemone generally spends most of its life in one place. It can
only catch food by waiting to see what swims by. When an unsuspecting
animal comes too close to the anemone's mouth, the anemone uses the
stinging cells in the tentacles that surround the mouth to shoot out tiny
poison threads. These paralyze the prey so it can be pulled into the
anemone's mouth. Sea anemones will eat practically anything that swims by.

Anemones can live up to 100 years. They are able to survive a long time
without food. When an anemone doesn't have enough food, it actually
diminishes in size so it will require less. Another unusual feature about the
sea anemone is that it does not have a skeleton. If the sea anemone is
threatened, it simply pulls in its tentacles so it looks like a rock or other
natural formation.

1. **Recognizing Words in Context**

   Find the word *diminishes* in the
   passage. One definition below is
   closest to the meaning of that word.
   One definition has the opposite or
   nearly opposite meaning. The
   remaining definition has a completely
   different meaning. Label the
   definitions C for *closest*, O for *opposite
   or nearly opposite*, and D for *different*.

   _____ a. increases

   _____ b. reshapes

   _____ c. decreases

2. **Distinguishing Fact from Opinion**

   Two of the statements below present
   facts, which can be proved correct.
   The other statement is an *opinion*,
   which expresses someone's thoughts
   or beliefs. Label the statements F for
   fact and O for *opinion*.

   _____ a. Anemones look exactly
   like plants.

   _____ b. Anemones do not have
   skeletons.

   _____ c. An anemone is an animal.

3. Keeping Events in Order

Label the statements below 1, 2, and 3 to show the order in which the events happen.

_____ a. A small fish swims near an anemone.

_____ b. An anemone's tentacles shoot out poison threads.

_____ c. The fish is paralyzed.

4. Making Correct Inferences

Two of the statements below are correct *inferences,* or reasonable guesses. They are based on information in the passage. The other statement is an incorrect, or faulty, inference. Label the statements C for *correct* inference and F for *faulty* inference.

_____ a. Anemones can be found in the tide pools that form along rocky ocean shores.

_____ b. Anemones live at least 100 years.

_____ c. The anemone's ability to shrink when it is not able to get much food helps it survive.

5. Understanding Main Ideas

One of the statements below expresses the main idea of the passage. One statement is too general, or too broad. The other explains only part of the passage; it is too narrow. Label the statements M for *main idea*, B for *too broad*, and N for *too narrow.*

_____ a. Sea anemones are sea animals with several unusual characteristics.

_____ b. Some sea animals look like plants.

_____ c. Sea anemones have stinging tentacles.

Correct Answers, Part A _____

Correct Answers, Part B _____

Total Correct Answers _____

Earthquakes are one of the least understood of nature's phenomena. Earthquakes can occur anywhere on the planet, but they are most common in a region called the Ring of Fire. This region runs along the perimeter of the Pacific Ocean, stretching from Japan to New Zealand and from Alaska to Chile. The strongest earthquake in North America occurred in Alaska in 1964. It registered 8.6 on the Richter scale.

The majority of earthquakes occur at tectonic plate boundaries. The rocky layer beneath Earth's soil is made up of about a dozen slowly moving tectonic plates. When one of these huge sections of rock pushes against another, it creates stress. The stress slowly builds up until sections of rock rupture and the plates suddenly shift, causing an earthquake. The point where the rock ruptures is called the focus. Places where plates have moved against each other are called faults. A dip-slip fault, also called a thrust fault, occurs when two plates move towards each other. One plate gets pushed up above the other. A strike-slip fault occurs when one plate is moving sideways along another. Most earthquakes result from a combination of dip-slip and strike-slip faults.

The point on Earth's surface that is directly above an earthquake's focus is called the epicenter. Energy is transmitted to Earth's surface by seismic waves. *Seismic* comes from the Greek word for "shaking." There are three types of seismic waves. The first waves to reach the surface are primary, or P, waves. Primary waves can travel through both solid and liquid matter. They compress and expand underground rock as they pass through. The next phase of waves consists of secondary, or S, waves. Secondary waves move more slowly and from side to side. These waves cause most of the structural damage in a quake. The third type of wave is the surface wave. Surface waves are created when the other wave types hit Earth's surface. Surface waves can travel long distances.

Earthquakes can destroy buildings; they can also cause landslides, tidal waves, and fires. Another danger arising from earthquakes is liquefaction. This occurs when loose soil shakes so much that its individual grains separate, leaving the ground they comprise in a soft, fluid state that can cause entire rows of buildings to collapse. People can minimize earthquake damage by not constructing buildings on loose soil. They also can use special construction methods to create buildings that can withstand shaking.

Reading Time _____

Recalling Facts

1. Earthquakes are most common in the area called
   - ❏ a. the Bermuda Triangle.
   - ❏ b. the Ring of Fire.
   - ❏ c. the Golden Crescent.

2. *Seismic* comes from the Greek word for
   - ❏ a. plating.
   - ❏ b. faulting.
   - ❏ c. shaking.

3. The first waves to hit Earth's surface in an earthquake are
   - ❏ a. P waves.
   - ❏ b. S waves.
   - ❏ c. X waves.

4. Two types of faults are
   - ❏ a. dip-slip and strike-slip.
   - ❏ b. thrust and crust.
   - ❏ c. thrust-slip and primary.

5. Most of the structural damage done by earthquakes is caused by
   - ❏ a. P waves.
   - ❏ b. Q waves.
   - ❏ c. S waves.

Understanding Ideas

6. Aside from the movement of tectonic plates, what might be another likely source of earthquakes?
   - ❏ a. volcanic eruptions
   - ❏ b. cruise missile explosions
   - ❏ c. collisions with asteroids

7. If an earthquake registering 9.0 on the Richter scale took place in Northern California, which of the following would most likely occur?
   - ❏ a. Florida would experience a tidal wave.
   - ❏ b. Tremors would be felt in Southern California.
   - ❏ c. Damage would be limited to the epicenter.

8. Which of the following cannot be concluded from the article?
   - ❏ a. The exact time an earthquake will occur can be predicted.
   - ❏ b. Earthquakes can occur in all parts of the world.
   - ❏ c. Earthquakes are natural occurrences.

9. If there were a major earthquake in San Jose, California, and it was felt as far away as Eugene, Oregon, the people in Eugene would be feeling
   - ❏ a. surface waves.
   - ❏ b. P waves.
   - ❏ c. S waves.

10. One can infer that the best place to construct a building to avoid earthquake damage would be on
    - ❏ a. a marshy area that has been filled in with soil.
    - ❏ b. on a thick layer of rock.
    - ❏ c. the edge of a beach.

Although severe earthquakes do occur more often in certain regions of the world than in others, quakes are actually happening continually in every region of Earth. This is because all regions of Earth lie above tectonic plates. Each year, Earth experiences about 3 million earthquakes. Some are so small that they are barely noticeable, while others may destroy entire villages.

The outer layer of Earth is known as the lithosphere. Tectonic plates form the foundation of the lithosphere. Tectonic plates under the ocean are called oceanic plates. Tectonic plates under land are called continental plates. Tectonic plates shift because of the movement of magma, molten rock from Earth's core. The majority of earthquakes occur along the edges of the oceanic and continental plates. Scientists have been able to ascertain the boundaries of oceanic plates by using satellites.

Tectonic plates vary in thickness. Oceanic plates are much thinner than continental plates. The most recently formed oceanic plates may be as thin as 15 kilometers (9 miles), whereas the oldest continental plates may be as thick as 200 kilometers (120 miles). Yet oceanic plates are as strong as continental plates, because they are made of denser rock.

Even the youngest tectonic plates are very old. Geologists believe they formed early in Earth's 4.6 billion–year history. Some plates disappear over time. They may sink beneath another plate and merge with the mantle.

1. **Recognizing Words in Context**

    Find the word *ascertain* in the passage. One definition below is closest to the meaning of that word. One definition has the opposite or nearly opposite meaning. The remaining definition has a completely different meaning. Label the definitions C for *closest*, O for *opposite or nearly opposite,* and D for *different.*

    _____ a. persuade

    _____ b. determine

    _____ c. confuse

2. **Distinguishing Fact from Opinion**

    Two of the statements below present *facts,* which can be proved correct. The other statement is an *opinion,* which expresses someone's thoughts or beliefs. Label the statements F for *fact* and O for *opinion.*

    _____ a. Continental plates lie beneath land.

    _____ b. A fault is a place where two plates have moved against each other.

    _____ c. People who live in areas above the borders of plates are taking foolish risks.

3. Keeping Events in Order

Label the statements below 1, 2, and 3 to show the order in which the events happen.

_____ a. Stress builds up between the plates.

_____ b. Two oceanic plates gradually come together.

_____ c. An earthquake occurs.

4. Making Correct Inferences

Two of the statements below are correct *inferences*, or reasonable guesses. They are based on information in the passage. The other statement is an incorrect, or faulty, inference. Label the statements C for *correct* inference and F for *faulty* inference.

_____ a. The thicker the plate, the greater its age.

_____ b. No matter where you live, you may experience an earthquake.

_____ c. All earthquakes can damage buildings.

5. Understanding Main Ideas

One of the statements below expresses the main idea of the passage. One statement is too general, or too broad. The other explains only part of the passage; it is too narrow. Label the statements M for *main idea*, B for *too broad*, and N for *too narrow*.

_____ a. Millions of earthquakes happen each year.

_____ b. Earthquakes are due to the movements of tectonic plates.

_____ c. Earthquakes and volcanic eruptions are related to activity deep beneath Earth's surface.

Correct Answers, Part A _____

Correct Answers, Part B _____

Total Correct Answers _____

Memory and the Brain

A human being's feelings, memories, and factual knowledge are all stored in the brain. The brain and the spinal cord together make up the central nervous system. The brain is capable of amazing things, and scientists are just beginning to understand how it works.

Human beings function by using their five senses: sight, hearing, taste, touch, and smell. All the information gathered by the senses is filtered through the brain for interpretation. The brain receives this sensory input through the spinal cord. Most of the brain's volume is dedicated to processing sensory data and initiating motor functions. Examples of motor functions that originate in the brain include walking, talking, and eating.

Memory is one of the most important functions of the brain. This function, too, relies on sensory information. Everything a person experiences using any of the five senses is converted into memory and stored in the brain.

There are two main types of memory: long-term memory and short-term memory. Long-term memory can also be divided into two types. One type is called procedural memory. This type of memory involves the use of learned skills, such as playing an instrument, driving a car, or typing. These memories allow a person to perform an action or procedure without consciously thinking about it. Procedural memories can be changed by new information or training. Another type of long-term memory is called declarative memory. This is where factual information is stored.

Short-term memory is used to record what is going on at the present time. For example, when a child is first taught how to tie a shoe, the experience is stored as short-term memory. As the child performs the process again and again, the information becomes part of the child's long-term procedural memory.

Memories operate in three basic steps. First, one of the five senses sends information to the brain in the form of nerve impulses. The brain then interprets these impulses and encodes them in a way that allows them to be stored with other memories. The third step is retrieval. This step involves accessing the stored memory or fact.

Scientists today are still researching and learning about the brain. Much remains undiscovered about this very important part of the human body. Advances in brain research will help people better understand human behavior. Research will also help with understanding more about memory and how information is processed.

Reading Time _____

Recalling Facts

1. The central nervous system consists of the brain and the
   - ❑ a. spinal cord.
   - ❑ b. eyes, ears, nose, mouth, and fingers.
   - ❑ c. heart.

2. The two main types of memory are long-term memory and
   - ❑ a. sensory memory.
   - ❑ b. intermediate memory.
   - ❑ c. short-term memory.

3. The brain receives information from the five senses in the form of
   - ❑ a. thoughts.
   - ❑ b. nerve impulses.
   - ❑ c. memories.

4. Walking is an example of
   - ❑ a. an involuntary activity.
   - ❑ b. sensory input.
   - ❑ c. a motor function.

5. The type of memory that is engaged when learning a new skill is called
   - ❑ a. procedural memory.
   - ❑ b. short-term memory.
   - ❑ c. declarative memory.

Understanding Ideas

6. In terms of its functions, the brain probably most closely resembles
   - ❑ a. a DVD player.
   - ❑ b. a computer.
   - ❑ c. a car engine.

7. When taking a test, a person would use the brain primarily for which function?
   - ❑ a. encoding
   - ❑ b. storing
   - ❑ c. retrieving

8. From the information in the article, one can assume that information sent to the brain by the five senses must travel through
   - ❑ a. the spinal cord.
   - ❑ b. the heart.
   - ❑ c. the eyes.

9. If a person cannot remember the first day of kindergarten, the experience was probably
   - ❑ a. stored in sensory memory but not long-term memory.
   - ❑ b. stored in short-term memory but not long-term memory.
   - ❑ c. encoded in long-term memory but stored in short-term memory.

10. An adult returns to a childhood park and begins to tell a story about what it felt like to play her first softball game there. This is most likely a function of
    - ❑ a. procedural memory.
    - ❑ b. declarative memory.
    - ❑ c. short-term memory.

Left Brain vs. Right Brain

The main part of the human brain is divided into two sections called hemispheres. These sections contain complementary abilities that are known as left-brain and right-brain traits.

Most people show a tendency toward either left-brain thinking or right-brain thinking. This means that a person has an affinity for one way of thinking about things over the other way. Left-brain people tend to be more logical and analytical. They are objective and have a tendency to look at things in terms of individual parts. They often excel in math and science. Right-brain people tend more toward creative pursuits. Writing or art may be their strengths. They are intuitive and subjective and are inclined to look at things as a whole.

In humans, body functions are cross-linked with the brain. The right side of the brain is responsible for controlling the actions of the left side of the body. The left side of the brain is responsible for controlling the actions of the right side of the body. Scientists have shown, however, that being left-handed or right-handed is not connected to being left-brain or right-brain.

Psychologists have designed tests that are intended to show whether a person is left-brain or right-brain. They have also determined that brain dominance can change over time. But the bottom line on brain dominance is that it is important to try to develop both sides of one's brain.

1. **Recognizing Words in Context**

    Find the word *affinity* in the passage. One definition below is closest to the meaning of that word. One definition has the opposite or nearly opposite meaning. The remaining definition has a completely different meaning. Label the definitions C for *closest*, O for *opposite or nearly opposite*, and D for *different*.

    _____ a. excellence

    _____ b. attraction

    _____ c. repulsion

2. **Distinguishing Fact from Opinion**

    Two of the statements below present *facts*, which can be proved correct. The other statement is an *opinion*, which expresses someone's thoughts or beliefs. Label the statements F for *fact* and O for *opinion*.

    _____ a. Left-brained people should become artists.

    _____ b. The main part of the human brain is divided into two hemispheres.

    _____ c. Body functions and the brain are cross-linked.

3. Keeping Events in Order

Label the statements below 1, 2, and 3 to show the order in which the events happen.

_____ a. A person accidentally touches a hot pan with the right hand.

_____ b. A person pulls back the right hand and grimaces in pain.

_____ c. A message is sent to the left side of the brain.

4. Making Correct Inferences

Two of the statements below are correct *inferences,* or reasonable guesses. They are based on information in the passage. The other statement is an incorrect, or faulty, inference. Label the statements C for *correct* inference and F for *faulty* inference.

_____ a. Most visual artists have a right-brain preference.

_____ b. A left-brain person will never become a right-brain person.

_____ c. Most mathematicians have a left-brain preference.

5. Understanding Main Ideas

One of the statements below expresses the main idea of the passage. One statement is too general, or too broad. The other explains only part of the passage; it is too narrow. Label the statements M for *main idea,* B for *too broad,* and N for *too narrow.*

_____ a. The two hemispheres of the brain have complementary characteristics.

_____ b. The brain consists of several different parts.

_____ c. Right-brained people tend to be artistic.

Correct Answers, Part A _____

Correct Answers, Part B _____

Total Correct Answers _____

Optical Illusions

Is seeing always believing? People are used to trusting that what they see is real, but sometimes their eyes play tricks on them. Actually, most of a person's normal vision is to some extent an illusion. For example, rainbows are not material objects, and parallel lines that stretch away from a person appear to converge on the horizon. When the moon is seen just above the horizon, it appears larger than it should. These are physical illusions, which means they are caused by the physical properties of light. The human brain tries to adapt to the complexities of the visual process, but there are limits to what it can make sense of.

The brain must interpret the information it receives from the eyes. The information takes the form of nerve impulses. Sometimes the impulses provide conflicting or incomplete information. Scientific experts are still trying to understand just what goes on in the eye-brain connection that causes optical illusions. Much of what they have learned about optical illusions has come from studying the brains of artists, because many artists strive to make two-dimensional art seem real.

When light travels through the eye, it is absorbed by photoreceptive cells on the retina. The images on the retina are flat images on a curved surface. It doesn't matter whether the image that is perceived is a two-dimensional painting or a three-dimensional mountain. Any one piece of a particular scene can be ambiguous or unclear. For example, if a passenger on a moving train looks out a window, the passenger may feel that he or she is not moving and the objects outside are.

Sometimes illusions are due to the brain's interpreting an image in more than one way. This is the basis for so-called three-dimensional pictures. When a person first looks at such a picture, it looks like a meaningless arrangement of patterns and colors. But if he or she spends time with the picture, the eyes may perceive a three-dimensional image within the picture. Some people are able to see the image if they try to look through the picture. Others repeatedly move toward the picture and away from it in order to see the image. What happens is that the brain is arranging elements of the picture in different ways to try to make sense of it. This shows the flexibility and sophistication of human vision and the brain in general.

Reading Time _____

Recalling Facts

1. Optical illusions are caused by
   - ❏ a. insufficient light.
   - ❏ b. three-dimensional objects.
   - ❏ c. misinterpretations by the brain.

2. The human eye works by taking light and turning it into
   - ❏ a. a two-dimensional image.
   - ❏ b. a three-dimensional image.
   - ❏ c. a photoreceptive cell.

3. Something that appears to be a material object but is not is a
   - ❏ a. moving train.
   - ❏ b. rainbow.
   - ❏ c. mountain.

4. Photoreceptive cells are located on the
   - ❏ a. cornea.
   - ❏ b. iris.
   - ❏ c. retina.

5. The surface of the retina is
   - ❏ a. flat.
   - ❏ b. curved.
   - ❏ c. angled.

Understanding Ideas

6. From the information in the article, one can infer that the human eye is connected to the brain by
   - ❏ a. arteries.
   - ❏ b. nerves.
   - ❏ c. air passages.

7. From the article, one can infer that
   - ❏ a. everyone perceives colors in the same way.
   - ❏ b. men see colors in the same way as women see colors.
   - ❏ c. the way that colors are perceived is partly a matter of interpretation.

8. What is one way artists can make two-dimensional images seem real?
   - ❏ a. use vivid colors rather than earth tones
   - ❏ b. make objects in the background smaller than objects in the foreground
   - ❏ c. put feeling into their work

9. The article suggests that once people understand that an object they are seeing is an optical illusion, the next time they see it they
   - ❏ a. won't recognize it.
   - ❏ b. are more likely to be able to identify it correctly.
   - ❏ c. are less likely to be able to identify it correctly.

10. From the passage, one can infer that
    - ❏ a. optical illusions are a normal part of the visual process.
    - ❏ b. highly intelligent people do not experience illusions.
    - ❏ c. anyone who sees an illusion needs a vision test.

What Is a Mirage?

The word *mirage* comes from the French word *mirer,* which means "to look at." Drivers who are traveling on a hot day sometimes report seeing a shaking, shimmering lake on the road ahead. This is a typical mirage. Another common mirage is experienced by people in the desert who believe they see a pool of water in the distance. Although mirages usually are seen in hot places, they also can take place in polar regions. For example, sailors in polar waters have claimed to see icebergs or other ships in low-lying clouds.

Mirages are caused by variations in the refractive index of the atmosphere. The atmosphere is made up of many different layers, each with its own temperature and density. A refractive index shows how much sunlight is distorted as it travels through the atmosphere. Extreme refraction variations often occur due to uneven heating of the air. Boundaries between irregular air temperatures can often act as a mirror, causing an illusion. The mirage of the lake on the road, for instance, is caused by the vast temperature difference between the hot air that is just above the road and the cooler air higher up.

People's states of mind can play a role in how they interpret a mirage. A person who is dying of thirst in the desert may be so desperate to see water that she or he interprets an area of wavy air as a pool.

1. Recognizing Words in Context

Find the word *distorted* in the passage. One definition below is closest to the meaning of that word. One definition has the opposite or nearly opposite meaning. The remaining definition has a completely different meaning. Label the definitions C for *closest,* O for *opposite or nearly opposite,* and D for *different.*

_____ a. distinct

_____ b. unclear

_____ c. bright

2. Distinguishing Fact from Opinion

Two of the statements below present *facts,* which can be proved correct. The other statement is an *opinion,* which expresses someone's thoughts or beliefs. Label the statements F for *fact* and O for *opinion.*

_____ a. *Mirage* comes from the French word *mirer.*

_____ b. Mirages are caused by temperature differences.

_____ c. People who see mirages tend to be foolish.

3. Keeping Events in Order

Label the statements below 1, 2, and 3 to show the order in which the events happen.

_____ a. The boundary between the hot and cool air acts as a mirror.

_____ b. An area of cool air comes into contact with an area of hot air.

_____ c. A person sees a mirage.

4. Making Correct Inferences

Two of the statements below are correct *inferences,* or reasonable guesses. They are based on information in the passage. The other statement is an incorrect, or faulty, inference. Label the statements C for *correct* inference and F for *faulty* inference.

_____ a. If the difference in air temperature is eliminated, the mirage goes away.

_____ b. A mirage is a natural phenomenon.

_____ c. Some mirages end up being actual pools of water.

5. Understanding Main Ideas

One of the statements below expresses the main idea of the passage. One statement is too general, or too broad. The other explains only part of the passage; it is too narrow. Label the statements M for *main idea,* B for *too broad,* and N for *too narrow.*

_____ a. Temperature can play a role in optical illusions.

_____ b. Mirages are optical illusions caused by variations in the refractive index of the atmosphere.

_____ c. The refractive index deals with the distortion of sunlight.

Correct Answers, Part A _____

Correct Answers, Part B _____

Total Correct Answers _____

25   A   The Dandelion

Each year homeowners in most parts of the United States battle to keep dandelions out of their lawns. Many people consider the dandelion to be a weed, but it can also be classified as a wild vegetable. The dandelion is also called swine's snout, priest's crown, and telltime. It is found in nearly every region of the Northern Hemisphere.

The dandelion has a thick taproot, which is a main root that reaches deep into the ground. The taproot is dark brown on the outside and milky white inside. If a gardener removes a dandelion from a lawn but leaves part of the taproot in the ground, the dandelion can grow back. A ring of narrow, shiny, dark green leaves rise from the taproot. The edges of the leaves of some types of dandelions are jagged like sharp teeth, and the word *dandelion* comes from the French phrase *dent de lion,* which means "lion's tooth." The stalk is hollow and produces a single yellow blossom. The blooms are sensitive to weather. When the sun is out, all parts of the flower stretch out to catch its rays, and as the sun sets, the whole head closes up. It also closes when rain falls.

Dandelion flowers produce large amounts of pollen and nectar. Many bees and other insects visit the dandelion to sip the nectar. The dandelion blooms from spring to late autumn, so it provides a good food source for bees. When the flower dies, it closes and the dead petals fall off. Soon the seeds mature and form the familiar white snowball-like cluster. The seeds detach very easily and are carried off by the wind.

Humans have used dandelions for many purposes, including medicinal ones. The first mention of using dandelions to make medicine is found in the works of Arabian physicians in the 10th and 11th centuries. Some benefits that have been attributed to the dandelion are lowering blood pressure, relieving acne, and treating anemia. When prepared properly, all parts of the dandelion can be used for food. Young dandelion leaves are sometimes used in salads, and older leaves can be boiled and eaten as a vegetable. Dried dandelion leaves can be used to make diet drinks. Dandelion coffee is prepared from the root. Some people consider dandelion coffee to be a healthful natural beverage because it does not irritate the digestive system the way regular coffee can.

Reading Time _____

Recalling Facts

1. A dandelion stalk produces.
   - ❏ a. two yellow flowers.
   - ❏ b. one white flower.
   - ❏ c. one yellow flower.

2. The dandelion can be classified as a
   - ❏ a. wild vegetable.
   - ❏ b. wild fruit.
   - ❏ c. domestic grain.

3. Dandelion seeds are transported most often by
   - ❏ a. water.
   - ❏ b. wind.
   - ❏ c. animals.

4. Dandelion coffee is made from the
   - ❏ a. leaves.
   - ❏ b. stem.
   - ❏ c. root.

5. Dandelion medicines were first mentioned by
   - ❏ a. Arabian physicians.
   - ❏ b. Greek scholars.
   - ❏ c. Roman scientists.

Understanding Ideas

6. From the article, one can conclude that the dandelion
   - ❏ a. is a major food source for people.
   - ❏ b. has both good and bad points.
   - ❏ c. is a useless weed.

7. When children blow on a dandelion "snowball" in a field, they are
   - ❏ a. dispersing nectar for the bees.
   - ❏ b. reducing the number of seeds that can be dispersed.
   - ❏ c. helping to disperse seeds.

8. One can conclude from this article that people have trouble removing dandelions from lawns because
   - ❏ a. of the plants' taproots.
   - ❏ b. people are lazy.
   - ❏ c. all of the seeds grow into adult plants.

9. If you saw dandelion flowers fold up in the middle of a spring day, you could assume that
   - ❏ a. seeds were about to appear.
   - ❏ b. rain was approaching.
   - ❏ c. harmful substances were in the air.

10. One can infer that foods made with dandelions should be made
    - ❏ a. by anybody.
    - ❏ b. only by chefs who have had years of training.
    - ❏ c. by people who know how to remove any harmful substances from the plants.

Natural Superstitions

Over time, many plants and animals have come to symbolize good fortune. One example is the acorn. In Scandinavian tradition, it is thought that an acorn placed on a windowsill, will cause Thor, the god of thunder and lightning, to spare that house from being struck by lightning. In another Scandinavian tradition, if an acorn falls when a person is standing under an oak tree, it is thought that she or he should pick it up, turn around three times, and make a wish. The acorn should then be placed on a windowsill to make the wish stronger.

Acorns are not the only plant parts that are associated with wishes' coming true. For example, if a person picks a blossom of Queen Anne's lace, holds it overhead, makes a wish, and tosses the blossom over his or her right shoulder without looking back, the wish will supposedly come true. The first ripe strawberry of the season is believed to be magical as well. Eat it, wish, and it is thought that the wish will be granted. Children have been making wishes with dandelions for centuries. If a person blows on the dandelion snowball and all the seeds come off, it is thought that the person's wish will come true.

1. **Recognizing Words in Context**

   Find the word *spare* in the passage. One definition below is closest to the meaning of that word. One definition has the opposite or nearly opposite meaning. The remaining definition has a completely different meaning. Label the definitions C for *closest*, O for *opposite or nearly opposite*, and D for *different*.

   _____ a. build

   _____ b. save

   _____ c. expose

2. **Distinguishing Fact from Opinion**

   Two of the statements below present *facts*, which can be proved correct. The other statement is an *opinion*, which expresses someone's thoughts or beliefs. Label the statements F for *fact* and O for *opinion*.

   _____ a. Scandinavian traditions associate acorns with good luck.

   _____ b. Making wishes is a waste of time.

   _____ c. Children use dandelions to make wishes.

3. Keeping Events in Order

Label the statements below 1, 2, and 3 to show the order in which the events happen.

_____ a. Two of the seeds remain on the plant.

_____ b. A child blows on the dandelion's seeds and makes a wish.

_____ c. A child sees a dandelion.

4. Making Correct Inferences

Two of the statements below are correct *inferences*, or reasonable guesses. They are based on information in the passage. The other statement is an incorrect, or faulty, inference. Label the statements C for *correct* inference and F for *faulty* inference.

_____ a. There is usually some solid logic behind superstitions.

_____ b. Throughout history there have been superstitions about items that bring good luck.

_____ c. An acorn may mean different things to people in different cultures.

5. Understanding Main Ideas

One of the statements below expresses the main idea of the passage. One statement is too general, or too broad. The other explains only part of the passage; it is too narrow. Label the statements M for *main idea*, B for *too broad*, and N for *too narrow*.

_____ a. Eating the first ripe strawberry of the season is thought to be good luck.

_____ b. Superstitions exist in many cultures.

_____ c. Some people associate certain plants with good luck.

Correct Answers, Part A _____

Correct Answers, Part B _____

Total Correct Answers _____

ANSWER KEY

READING RATE GRAPH

COMPREHENSION SCORE GRAPH

COMPREHENSION SKILLS PROFILE GRAPH

ANSWER KEY

1A	1. b	2. c	3. a	4. c	5. c	6. b	7. b	8. a	9. c	10. a
1B	1. D, C, O	2. F, O, F	3. 2, 3, 1	4. F, C, C	5. M, N, B
2A	1. b	2. a	3. a	4. a	5. c	6. b	7. b	8. a	9. a	10. a
2B	1. C, D, O	2. F, O, F	3. 3, 2, 1	4. C, F, C	5. N, M, B
3A	1. c	2. a	3. c	4. b	5. c	6. c	7. a	8. a	9. c	10. b
3B	1. C, D, O	2. O, F, F	3. 3, 1, 2	4. C, C, F	5. B, M, N
4A	1. c	2. b	3. a	4. c	5. b	6. b	7. c	8. a	9. c	10. a
4B	1. D, O, C	2. O, F, F	3. 1, 3, 2	4. C, F, C	5. B, N, M
5A	1. c	2. a	3. c	4. b	5. a	6. c	7. a	8. a	9. b	10. a
5B	1. C, O, D	2. O, F, F	3. 3, 2, 1	4. C, F, C	5. B, M, N
6A	1. c	2. a	3. a	4. c	5. b	6. c	7. b	8. a	9. c	10. a
6B	1. O, C, D	2. O, F, F	3. 2, 3, 1	4. C, F, C	5. M, B, N
7A	1. b	2. c	3. b	4. a	5. b	6. a	7. a	8. b	9. c	10. b
7B	1. C, O, D	2. F, O, F	3. 3, 1, 2	4. C, C, F	5. B, N, M
8A	1. b	2. c	3. c	4. a	5. b	6. b	7. c	8. a	9. a	10. c
8B	1. O, D, C	2. O, F, F	3. 2, 1, 3	4. C, C, F	5. N, B, M
9A	1. c	2. b	3. c	4. b	5. a	6. c	7. a	8. b	9. b	10. a
9B	1. O, C, D	2. F, O, F	3. 2, 3, 1	4. C, C, F	5. M, B, N
10A	1. b	2. c	3. a	4. b	5. c	6. c	7. b	8. a	9. b	10. a
10B	1. O, D, C	2. O, F, F	3. 1, 3, 2	4. C, F, C	5. B, M, N
11A	1. a	2. c	3. b	4. b	5. a	6. b	7. a	8. b	9. c	10. b
11B	1. O, C, D	2. F, O, F	3. 1, 2, 3	4. F, C, C	5. M, B, N
12A	1. c	2. b	3. a	4. c	5. b	6. c	7. a	8. b	9. b	10. a
12B	1. C, O, D	2. O, F, F	3. 2, 1, 3	4. F, C, C	5. B, M, N
13A	1. c	2. a	3. b	4. a	5. c	6. b	7. c	8. b	9. b	10. c
13B	1. D, C, O	2. F, O, F	3. 2, 1, 3	4. F, C, C	5. B, N, M

14A	1. c	2. b	3. a	4. b	5. c	6. c	7. b	8. b	9. a	10. b
14B	1. O, D, C		2. F, F, O		3. 2, 3, 1		4. C, F, C		5. N, B, M	
15A	1. b	2. c	3. a	4. b	5. a	6. a	7. c	8. c	9. b	10. a
15B	1. C, D, O		2. F, F, O		3. 3, 2, 1		4. F, C, C		5. M, N, B	
16A	1. c	2. a	3. b	4. b	5. a	6. b	7. b	8. a	9. c	10. a
16B	1. D, C, O		2. F, O, F		3. 1, 3, 2		4. C, F, C		5. N, B, M	
17A	1. b	2. a	3. a	4. b	5. c	6. b	7. b	8. a	9. b	10. c
17B	1. D, C, O		2. O, F, F		3. 2, 1, 3		4. F, C, C		5. B, M, N	
18A	1. c	2. a	3. b	4. c	5. c	6. c	7. b	8. a	9. a	10. b
18B	1. O, D, C		2. F, O, F		3. 1, 3, 2		4. F, C, C		5. N, M, B	
19A	1. b	2. a	3. b	4. a	5. c	6. a	7. b	8. b	9. c	10. a
19B	1. C, D, O		2. F, F, O		3. 3, 2, 1		4. F, C, C		5. N, M, B	
20A	1. b	2. c	3. a	4. b	5. c	6. b	7. a	8. c	9. b	10. a
20B	1. D, O, C		2. F, O, F		3. 1, 3, 2		4. C, C, F		5. B, M, N	
21A	1. b	2. a	3. c	4. a	5. b	6. c	7. a	8. c	9. b	10. b
21B	1. O, D, C		2. O, F, F		3. 1, 2, 3		4. C, F, C		5. M, B, N	
22A	1. b	2. c	3. a	4. a	5. c	6. a	7. b	8. a	9. a	10. b
22B	1. D, C, O		2. F, F, O		3. 2, 1, 3		4. C, C, F		5. N, M, B	
23A	1. a	2. c	3. b	4. c	5. b	6. b	7. c	8. a	9. b	10. b
23B	1. D, C, O		2. O, F, F		3. 1, 3, 2		4. C, F, C		5. M, B, N	
24A	1. c	2. a	3. b	4. c	5. b	6. b	7. c	8. b	9. b	10. a
24B	1. O, C, D		2. F, F, O		3. 2, 1, 3		4. C, C, F		5. B, M, N	
25A	1. c	2. a	3. b	4. c	5. a	6. b	7. c	8. a	9. b	10. c
25B	1. D, C, O		2. F, O, F		3. 3, 2, 1		4. F, C, C		5. N, B, M	

READING RATE

Put an X on the line above each lesson number to show your reading time and words-per-minute rate for that lesson.

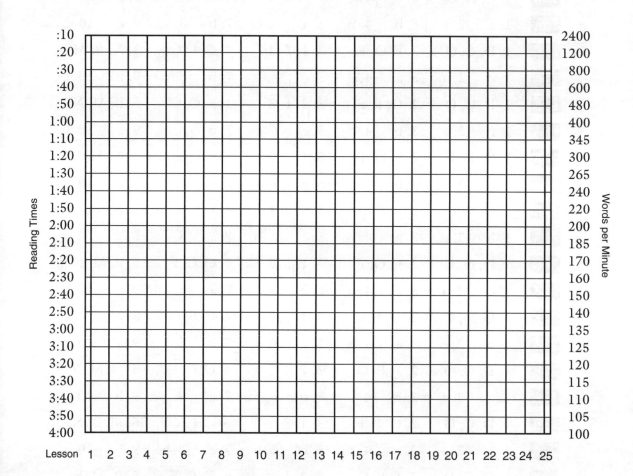

COMPREHENSION SCORE

Put an X on the line above each lesson number to indicate your total correct answers and comprehension score for that lesson.

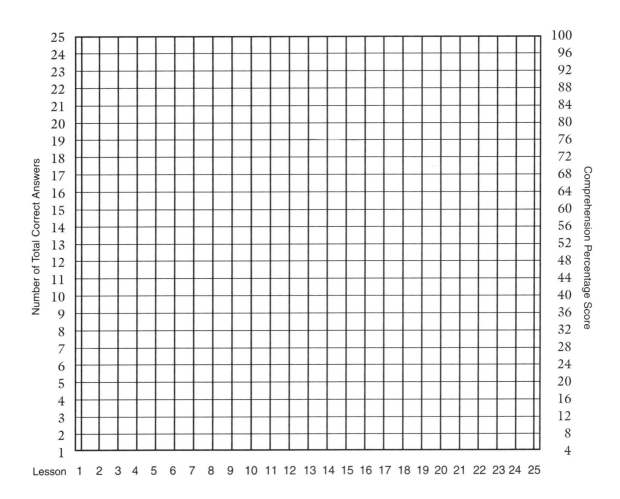

COMPREHENSION SKILLS PROFILE

Put an X in the box above each question type to indicate an incorrect reponse to any part of that question.

	Recognizing Words in Context	Distinguishing Fact from Opinion	Keeping Events in Order	Making Correct Inferences	Understanding Main Ideas
Lesson 1					
2					
3					
4					
5					
6					
7					
8					
9					
10					
11					
12					
13					
14					
15					
16					
17					
18					
19					
20					
21					
22					
23					
24					
25					